Those 'impossible' events you hear about, like UFOs, mysterious disappearances, Bigfoot ... are they real? The answer is a resounding 'Yes!' Sutherly combines the skills of a skeptical investigative reporter with decades of personal involvement with anomalous phenomena and the leading paranormal researchers. The result is a trustworthy and sophisticated handbook of the unexplained.

— Robert J. Durant
Ufologist and anomalist

There's something strange going on in our world. Consider, if you will, the "Thing" of Sheep's Hill, that unnerved the residents of Pottstown, Pennsylvania, by stealing poultry, screaming deep into the night, and making twenty-foot leaps to avoid gunfire. Or the puzzling radioactive object that crashed in a frozen pond in New Hampshire, melting the ice and sending the state government into a tailspin. Or the prehistoric birds and dinosaurs that are still reported to roam the Earth.

These mysteries make us acutely aware of how little we understand our world and the universe beyond. Turn the page—and prepare to come face-to-face with the unknown.

About the Author

Curt Sutherly is a professional journalist who has studied and written about unexplained phenomena for over twenty years. His writing has appeared in newspapers and magazines across the country. An active interest in wildlife and natural history, combined with his background as an Air Force sergeant and his investigations of the paranormal, have given Curt a unique perspective from which to write this book. A native of Pennsylvania, Curt is currently a federal civil servant for the Department of Air Force.

To Write to the Author

If you wish to contact the author or would like more information about this book, please write to him in care of Llewellyn Worldwide and we will forward your request. Both the author and publisher appreciate hearing from you and learning of your enjoyment of this book and how it has helped you. Llewellyn Worldwide cannot guarantee that every letter written to the author can be answered, but all will be forwarded. Please write to:

Curt Sutherly
c/o Llewellyn Worldwide
P.O. Box 64383, Dept. K699-8
St. Paul, MN 55164-0383, U.S.A.

Enclose a self-addressed, stamped envelope for reply, or $1.00 to cover costs. If outside the U.S.A., enclose international postal reply coupons.

Free Catalog from Llewellyn

For more than ninety years Llewellyn has brought its readers knowledge in the fields of metaphysics and human potential. Learn about the newest books in spiritual guidance, natural healing, astrology, occult philosophy, and more. Enjoy book reviews, New Age articles, a calendar of events, plus current advertised products and services. To get your free copy of Llewellyn's New Worlds, send your name and address to:

Llewellyn's New Worlds of Mind and Spirit
P.O. Box 64383, Dept. K699-8
St. Paul, MN 55164-0383, U.S.A.

FATE Presents:

STRANGE ENCOUNTERS

UFOS, ALIENS & MONSTERS AMONG US

Curt Sutherly

1996
Llewellyn Publications
St. Paul, Minnesota, 55164-0383, U.S.A.

FIRST EDITION
Second Printing, 1996

Cover design: Maria Mazzara
Cover art: Martin Cannon
Book design and layout: Mark Lazar
Editing: Mark Lazar and Deb Gruebele

Library of Congress Cataloging-in-Publication Data
Sutherly, Curt, 1950–
    Strange encounters : UFOs, aliens, & monsters
among us / Curt Sutherly. -- 1st ed.
        p.   cm. -- (Fate presents)
    Includes bibliographical references (p.).
    ISBN 1–56718–699–8 (trade pbk.)
    1. Human alien encounters. I. Title. II. Series
BF2050.S88   1996
001.9'4--dc20   96–16994
                                                CIP

Printed in the United States of America

Llewellyn Publications
A Division of Llewellyn Worldwide, Ltd.
P.O. Box 64383, St. Paul, MN 55164-0383

About the FATE Presents Series

Since 1948, FATE magazine has brought true, documented reports of the strange and unusual to readers around the world. For more than four decades, FATE has reported on such subjects as UFOs and space aliens, Bigfoot, the Loch Ness monster, ESP, psychic powers, divination, ghosts and poltergeists, startling new scientific theories and breakthroughs, real magic, near-death and out-of-body experiences, survival after death, witches and witchcraft, and many other topics that will astound your imagination.

FATE has revealed the fakers and the frauds and examined the events and people with powers that defy explanation. When you read it in FATE, you can be sure that the information is certified and factual.

One of the things that makes FATE special is the wide variety of authors who write for it. Some of them have numerous books to their credit and are highly respected in their fields of speciality. Others are plain folks—whose lives have crossed over into the world of the paranormal.

Now Llewellyn is publishing a series of books bearing the FATE name. You hold one such book in your hands. The topic of this book may be one of any of the subjects we've described or a variety of them. It may be a collection of authenticated articles by unknown writers or a book by an author of world-renown.

There is one thing of which you can be assured: the occurrences described in this book are absolutely accurate and took place as reported. Now even more people will be able to marvel at, be shocked by, and enjoy true reports of the strange and unknown.

Other Books in the FATE Presents Series

Dedicated to the memory of my mother,
Mildred Mary Sutherly,
and to my father,
Curtis Simon Sutherly

Acknowledgements

The act of writing this book took a year of my available time, but the content—the material used—was researched and collected during the past twenty-five years. I am indebted to many during those years for their assistance and inspiration. Among those who contributed are the following: Rick and Carol Hilberg, Robert J. Durant, Gene Steinberg, Robert Warth, Allan J. Manak, Loren Coleman, Jerome Clark, James W. Moseley, Robert Lyman, Jr., Lucius Farish, Allen H. Greenfield, Betty Hill, Stan Gordon, Larry Kusche, Dr. Charles L. Wiedemann, J. Richard Greenwell, Stanton T. Friedman, Wayne VanDine, Helen McGinnis, John A. Keel, Philip J. Klass, John R. Lindermuth, Major General (retired) John C. McWhorter, Jr., Kevin D. Randle, Mark Chorvinsky, Edward Biebel, Brad Steiger, Nancy Gatch Svien, Eleanor Hoaglan, Geneva Hagen, Roy Jones, Ronald L. Kaylor, and Dick Welsh.

I would also like to thank Jim Connor of *Apprise* magazine, Mike Toth of *Sports Afield*, Paul Baker and Susan Moyer of the *Daily News* in Lebanon, Pennsylvania, as well as Cedric Kurtz, Rob McNamee and Walt Long, all formerly of the *Daily News*. At one time or another each has been my editor, and their talent and expertise did much to spur my growth as a writer.

Another who deserves special thanks is Floyd Murray, an outstanding Fortean investigator who has long labored behind the scenes near Philadelphia, providing others with the benefit of his research and understanding. Floyd has been friend and confidant, and without him this book most likely would not have been written.

I should also like to acknowledge ufologist Robert S. Easley of Cleveland, who befriended me at my very first UFO convention more than twenty-five years ago and who has remained my friend ever since; and Glenn and Danita Wampler, and Jim and Tammy Snyder, good friends all who provided help and encouragement and long evenings of discussion; Jim and Paula Rhule and Chris and Marina Dullnig, who are part of my "Maryland family," who agreed to the somewhat daunting task of reading an early draft of the manuscript and who offered many helpful suggestions; Cheryl Bodan and Joe Kosack of the Pennsylvania Game Commission, for their research assistance; Joan Thompson, for encouragement and long friendship; Mike Polinski, who witnessed the contract and was forced to put up with my intermittent concerns about the book; Deb Gruebele and Mark Lazar, my editors on this project; as well as Nan Skovran in acquisitions, Andrea Godwin in the publicity department, and everyone else at Llewellyn.

Finally, my heartfelt thanks to Kristie, Dori and Donna, my sisters, and Tim, my brother-in-law, for their love and encouragement.

C.S.

Contents

Foreword

The man is wisest who, like Socrates,
knows that his wisdom is worth nothing.

The words were written by the Greek philosopher Plato, and since his death in the year 347 B.C., the sum of human knowledge has grown immeasurably. And yet, Plato's words remain true. Our wisdom, our knowledge, is nothing. Smart as we think we are, arrogant as we often are, we remain surrounded by the unknown and thwarted by the unknowable.

I've spent a fair amount of time in pursuit of the unknown—writing about various phenomena that defy conventional wisdom or explanation. In the course of this, I've sometimes felt very near to an understanding of some particular strange event or occurrence. But at other times I've felt like an imbecile ... as though I knew nothing at all.

The only son and the oldest (by several years) of four siblings, I grew up a voracious reader. One of the books I read at an early age was an inexpensive paperback entitled *The Book of the Damned*. The author was a man named Charles Hoy Fort, and in the opening lines he explained his title. He said, "By the damned, I mean the excluded. We shall have a procession of data that Science has excluded."

Fort explored such diverse mysteries as eerie lights and strange aerial objects, black rains and lake monsters, lost planets and strange ancient artifacts, to mention a very few. And throughout it all, he attacked science for insisting on ignoring these mysteries. "Dogmatic Science," he called it. Eventually he wrote three other titles dealing with strange phenomena: *Lo!*, *New Lands*, and *Wild Talents* (the last published shortly after his death). Fort wrote with humor and acid wit, and was something of a philosopher besides. Plato and Fort probably would have gotten on famously, had they lived in the same era.

Fort died on May 3, 1932, at the age of fifty-seven. He died unappreciated and, I suspect, lonely, in part because of his insistence on attacking scientific dogma. But what he lacked in life was granted in death; appreciation and audience came to him posthumously. His books have been devoured by generations of readers recognizing the challenge of his words.

Fort's philosophy was to accept nothing, question everything. He would say, if alive today, "Look carefully at the world around you, and reexamine what you think you know."

Without a doubt Fort influenced my early thinking. I read everything I could find on "Fortean" phenomena, and continued doing so for several years. There came a time, however, when one particular Fortean subject fascinated me more than the rest: the subject of unidentified flying objects or UFOs. By the late 1960s this interest had grown quite strong, coinciding with my enlistment in the United States Air Force. This was also around the time I discovered the writings of John A. Keel.

A veteran journalist, John had trekked through the Orient in the 1950s, sleuthing out the mystery and magic of faraway lands. His experience resulted in a book, *Jadoo*, published in 1957. Back in the states in the 1960s, he began a long-term investigation of the UFO phenomenon. (He once said, "I thought I was smart enough to figure it all out.") Several books and countless articles resulted, and in each John made it abundantly clear that he doubted the conventional wisdom (among those who believed at all) that UFOs were alien spacecraft.

In 1972, John and I met in Washington, D.C., where he was working as a consultant for the Department of Health, Education, and Welfare. At the time I was beginning to entertain my own doubts that UFOs were extraterrestrial spacecraft. But the UFO issue was only part of the reason I wanted to meet him. To me, John was something of a hero. I admired him. His skill as a writer, his wit, and his narrative ability were standards by which I determined to measure my own early writing.

I was discharged from the military in September 1972. In November of that year my first freelance story appeared, published in a daily newspaper. The story was a travel piece, but it also contained a warning about the consequences of overpopulation as well as elements of Fortean mystery. In December 1972, I came very close to death: a car crash shattered my face and put me in a hospital. Long weeks passed before I was healthy enough to return to the everyday world.

For a time I worked odd jobs while simultaneously moving deeper into the study of UFOs. I investigated dozens of reported sightings, interviewed countless witnesses, and wrote about all of it. I was also, by then, beginning to spend weekends at the New Jersey farm of the late Ivan Sanderson.

A zoologist and writer, Ivan was founder of the Society for the Investigation of the Unexplained (SITU), then headquartered at his farm. He had traveled widely in his life, seeking out new plant and animal species for botanical gardens and national zoos. He had also written a good many books, mostly about wildlife and the natural sciences, but others concerned Fortean matters, including UFOs.

As a zoologist, Ivan was interested early on in the abominable snowman of the Himalayas, leading to his 1961 book, *Abominable Snowmen: Legend Come To Life*. He was curious about many things and that curiosity, along with a suggestion by the crypto-zoologist Loren Coleman (also a student of Fort), resulted in the eventual formation of SITU. Because the society was headquartered at the Sanderson farm, many of Ivan's zoological buddies inevitably found themselves assisting, one way or another, in its operation.

In 1972, I was making my first trip to the farm, the last mile or so of which followed an unmarked, unpaved, country road with many diverging paths. I'd been forewarned during a phone conversation that I would never find the place without an escort, and was told that someone from the society would meet me at a particular location. I arrived a bit early, but soon a station wagon drove up bearing SITU markings. A man got out of the car. He approached, grinned, and stuck out his hand: "My name is Ryhiner," he said. "Pete Ryhiner. If you have trouble recalling that, just think of rhinoceros."

Ryhiner was a professional animal collector and a longtime friend and associate of Ivan's. He was also, as I found out, a gourmet cook trained in Switzerland. That night he prepared a veritable feast attended by Ivan and Alma Sanderson, myself, and several friends. During dinner, Ivan regaled us with stories of his misspent youth. Afterward, I was recruited to assist in scrubbing the pots and pans literally blackened by Ryhiner while cooking.

While these stories are amusing to recall, what I remember most about my visits to Ivan's farm were the discussions he and I had about writing. Ivan was one of two writers I have known who could produce a lengthy, printable story first draft, no revisions. (John R. Lindermuth, a former newspaper colleague, was the other.) Ivan wrote on an old manual typewriter with a continuous roll of paper fixed over the machine. When the story or book was completed, he would cut the roll into pages and submit them to his publisher. He wrote in the same way he spoke—an easy, often folksy speech that anyone could follow and enjoy. During our conversations he encouraged me to maximize my own potential as a writer, even though at the time I was barely a novice.

I vividly recall the night Ivan asked me to become the resident caretaker of his farm. In exchange, he offered to serve as my mentor in matters of writing as well as in the natural sciences and other disciplines at his command. When I later declined, Alma, dying of cancer, urged me to reconsider. She did so in private, without consulting Ivan, and I'll never forget the pain in her eyes. Being a foolish young man, I failed to accept even then.

Following Alma's death, Ivan remarried. On February 19, 1973, at sixty-two, he too succumbed to

cancer. With his death, others took the reins of the
society, among them Robert C. Warth, Steven
Mayne, and Marty Wiegler. For a brief time, John
Keel was editor-in-chief of *Pursuit*, SITU's journal.
He in turn appointed me senior writer—a circum-
stance that lasted about a year.

With the new pecking order established, Keel
took off for Scandinavia to gather information on a
long-running and widespread UFO flap. At about the
same time a new and talented researcher came
along. Out of respect for the man and the friendship
we shared, I'll not use his true name. Instead, I'll call
him Raymond.

Like many others, Raymond had a strong interest in the UFO phenomenon. He was a consummate
writer, his talent evident in articles published in *Pursuit*, *Fate*, and similar journals. His instincts were
sharp and his mind extremely quick. Within a few
months he made a transition that had taken others
years to make if they made it at all: he dismissed the
prevailing belief that UFOs are extraterrestrial spacecraft and began working under the assumption that
something far more odd and complex is at work. But
his sharp mind and intuitive grasp were, I fear, also
his undoing.

What some of us failed to take into account was the
potential for heightened emotional and psychological stress. For Raymond and a number of others,
myself included, the stress arising from the unre-
lenting (and often undisciplined) study of UFOs was
worsened by a belief that the phenomenon was
more metaphysical than physical. To accept, on our
terms, the occurrence of UFOs was to accept the
notion that all of reality originates on a mental or

metaphysical plane, and is limited only by our sub-conscious beliefs.

In any event, we became obsessed with this view. At the same time, bizarre occurrences became almost commonplace. For Raymond, it became a nightmare.

The man spent more and more time absorbed in trying to prove our "solution" to the UFO puzzle. From all outward signs, this resulted in problems in his home. (He was married and had a beautiful family.) His stress level soared and small wonder: UFOs and strange creatures were suddenly everywhere within driving distance of his home. In the creature department, hairy man-beasts and even lizardmen were reported. Mysterious screams and sounds issued from area forests. Nocturnal lights in the sky (and on the ground) were spotted routinely. Mutilations of animals began to occur, serving to intensify the already rampant fear and suspicion. (In one of the worst of these, a farmer's rabbits were removed from their pens and killed. Some were torn apart. Others were crushed as if by huge powerful hands; the broken bodies were left lying atop the pens.)

In my rented cottage some two hundred miles away, the telephone became an instrument of great annoyance. My conversations were routinely interrupted by strange sounds and third-party voices. Important files began to disappear. Outside the cottage, my car developed a talent for turning on its own headlights.

In one instance, I drove to a nearby village to purchase groceries. While in the store, my car lights switched on. It was midday and the car was in full view from a window of the store. I switched off the lights when I returned to the vehicle, and made a second stop en route home. When I again returned, the lights were back on. I switched them off a second time and drove home, feeling exasperated. Inside the cottage, the telephone began to ring. When I answered, there was no response. As I stood cursing at the phone, I looked out at my car; the headlights were back on.

Raymond's own difficulty, meanwhile, was compounded by his fear for his family. He expressed this in one of the last letters I received from him. He said, "You and I know that most (or all) of these phenomena do indeed originate in the unconscious mind. I am beginning to worry about what might happen in or around my own home. I know of no way to shake such 'thoughts' from my unconscious mind, of course, so I feel frustrated in my desire to stop the events short of my property line."

His fears were realized soon after, when huge, three-toed creature tracks were found outside his home. I recall sitting in Raymond's living room while he went to another room to retrieve a cast of one of the tracks. The cast was enormous and quite deep, and sent shivers down my spine. The "animal" that made it would have had to weigh one thousand pounds or more.

Not long after, I received the final letter. In it, Raymond severed all ties, expressing a desire for no further contact. I recognized in his words the panic and dismay of an embattled man. Others, too, received the letter, or one similar. Several months later I also withdrew from the field.

I was, by then, a full-time newspaper reporter, anxious to develop my skills. In addition, I was uneasy over Raymond's departure and I sensed a growing unhappiness among other formerly enthusiastic researchers. So I bowed out and went on to write "general assignment" stories about local government, crime, and community events, and finally, to create a weekly outdoor column.

For ten years I stayed away from Fortean phenomena. I began to travel. In Puerto Rico, I explored old San Juan and entered the remote rain forests. In the desert Southwest, I climbed through ancient ruins and walked modern cities. In the remote forests of northern Quebec, I watched the delighted smile of a Cree Indian boy at his first taste of spiced sausage. In the Midwest, I camped with two young men who had just dodged a tornado.

I fell in love. I married and divorced, and I paid a visit to Hell. When I returned, I dusted off my old leather jacket and again changed my career. Then I received a phone call. Over the ensuing months, a series of freelance articles followed, the first I'd written on any Fortean subject in a decade—which brings me to the present and the book you hold.

I have no pretensions about what I have written. I offer no shocking new insights or arguments, no brilliant new explanations for any of the mysteries I have chosen to describe. I merely bring a different perspective and, perhaps, a touch of journalistic dispassion.

In the end, books are written to inform or to entertain, or both. If I have accomplished a little of both, then I am satisfied.

Curt Sutherly
Indiantown Gap, Pennsylvania
December 1993

Mystery in the Sky, and Beyond

When I say that flying saucers are a subset of larger issues, I mean that they are not a self-contained puzzle to be solved. They are just one piece of a larger, more complicated puzzle.
                                                                    —Peter Kor

Chapter One:

"They don't know a damn thing ..."

Throughout the world, 1947 was a spectacular year in aviation. New records and standards for flight were established, and just as quickly broken.

At Muroc Field (now Edwards AFB) in California, a group of Air Force aviators and technicians pursued an "impossible" goal and succeeded—they broke the sound barrier. One of their number was a war ace named Chuck Yeager, who was also a gifted test pilot. The craft was a small orange rocket plane designed by Bell Aircraft: the X–1.

The air-launched X–1 was hauled aloft by a B–29 bomber. At twenty thousand feet, the machine and pilot were dropped and the rockets ignited. The first test flight was conducted in December 1946. The pilot was a civilian, Chalmers "Slick" Goodlin. But it was Yeager at the controls on October 14, 1947—the day the barrier fell. Forty years later, he related in his book *Press On* that what was most remarkable about the flight "was what didn't happen. We didn't disintegrate, didn't 'hit the wall,' didn't even feel a bump when we went supersonic."

Thanks to military secrecy, nine months would pass before the outside world knew of Yeager's accomplishment.

While all this was going on the Northrop Corporation was completing development of a "flying wing" for the fledgling United States Air Force.[1] An early prototype, the XB-35, flew in June 1946, and a jet version, the YB-49, flew the following year. The YB-49 crashed in 1948 while being tested by Capt. Glenn Edwards (Muroc Field was renamed in his honor). A second B-49 burned during a taxiing accident, and a third was scrapped. A number of others were ordered destroyed on the assembly line. Years later, the late John K. Northrop claimed the flying wing program was deliberately canceled by the secretary of the Air Force, Stuart Symington, for political reasons and not for technical problems as was reported at the time.

While the Air Force was still testing the flying wing, the United States Navy was working on its own version: a prop-driven, circular machine, the XF5U-1, otherwise known as the "flying flapjack." The aircraft was designed to ascend vertically and hover as well as fly horizontally. The test program was carried out at Muroc Field under security so tight even the Air Force was kept in the dark. But in the end the Navy's flapjack went the way of the Northrop wing, pushed aside in favor of more conventional jet-powered aircraft.

Elsewhere, on California's Long Beach Harbor on November 2, millionaire aircraft designer Howard Hughes piloted a machine many said would never fly: the world's largest flying boat, known affectionately as the "Spruce Goose." With a 320-foot wingspan and measuring 219 feet, the 190-ton Goose raised seventy feet during a one thousand-yard test run.

Afterward, Hughes thumbed his nose at a skeptical world and hangared the aircraft, which he never again flew.

The following month, on December 10, aviatrix Jacqueline Cochran piloted her P–51 Mustang over a measured one hundred-kilometer course at an average speed of nearly 470 miles per hour, establishing a new record. She added to her achievement the following year, setting a record pace over a one thousand-kilometer course at an average speed of 431 miles per hour.

Throughout this period the changes in aircraft design were incessant and ongoing—a result of rigorous testing of new airframes mated to postwar jet engine technology.

Enter a flier named Kenneth Arnold. Like others during this period, he made it into the record books. He is listed in *Air Facts and Feats—A Record of International Aerospace Achievement*. But unlike all the others, Arnold was not a test pilot or a stunt flier.

A private pilot and owner of a fire-control equipment company in Boise, Idaho, Arnold was aloft in his single-engine plane on the afternoon of June 24, 1947, assisting in a search for a crashed C–46 Marine transport. The day was sunny and clear—a beautiful day, he would later recall.

The veteran pilot had departed Chehalis (Washington) Airport at about 2:00 P.M., and was in the vicinity of Mount Rainier when he was surprised by a flash that reflected from the side of his airplane. When a second flash occurred, Arnold located the source: nine objects gleaming in the sun as they flew south from the direction of Mount Baker, flying in echelon formation, sweeping back and forth among the peaks.

Amazed, Arnold nonetheless had enough presence of mind to triangulate the speed of the objects as they passed between Rainier and Mount Adams, forty-five miles to the south. His computations suggested the impossible. The objects were traveling at about sixteen hundred miles per hour, far faster than any known aircraft—much faster even than the secret Bell X–1 which, in exceeding Mach 1 later in the year, would travel at about seven hundred miles per hour. (The speed of sound is 660 miles per hour at forty thousand feet.)

Arnold described the motion of the objects as unusual, like "speedboats on rough water," or "like a saucer … if you skipped it across water." The sighting thrust him into the spotlight. Unwillingly, he became a celebrity—the first pilot to officially report and document the sighting of UFOs.

Arnold's sighting seemed to trigger a national epidemic. People everywhere began reporting strange aerial objects. There were even unconfirmed reports of crashed discs in the desert Southwest, causing a storm of controversy that continues today (we'll focus on this in a later chapter).

For a time, political and military leaders regarded the rash of "flying saucer" reports as a form of postwar hysteria. They decided it would eventually fade, but it never did. Today the sightings continue, with many reports made by sane, sober people whose testimony would be acceptable in a court of law, but who nonetheless remain open to media ridicule and public harassment.

It was no different for Ken Arnold. He was plagued by individuals who hounded him for details, and by news reporters who wanted his "story" but who knew little or nothing about the UFO phenomenon.

As a journalist, I had the distinction of being one of the last persons to ever interview Ken Arnold. As such it wasn't much of an interview, conducted briefly and by telephone. But it was substantially more than anyone had gotten from the man in a long time.

The interview was conducted on June 24, 1976,[2] the anniversary of Arnold's sighting. At the time, I was in touch with UFO and Fortean researchers throughout the country while earning a meager living as a writer of magazine articles and occasional newspaper copy. Most of the time I was broke and the money I received from sales of stories, when it arrived (the checks were almost always overdue), was used to finance the pursuit of new mysteries in new locations. Because I was young, barely an adult at twenty-five, travel and adventure seemed more important than regular meals and a roof over my head.

At some point during all of this I obtained a copy of a book called *The Coming of the Saucers*, co-written by Ken Arnold and the late Ray Palmer. The story, told in a simple, straightforward narrative, recounted Arnold's experiences in the weeks after his Mount Rainier sighting. It was a hair-raising account—an adventure straight out of early pulp science fiction. I was fascinated, but also suspicious: Palmer had been a publisher of science fiction, so how much of the book was fact and how much was fiction?

I began to inquire around, trying to determine the whereabouts of Ken Arnold. But my various contacts were unable to help. "Isn't Arnold dead?" someone suggested. Another said he had heard that Arnold and family had moved to Australia to escape the constant harassment from reporters and UFO enthusiasts. The truth, as I discovered, was far simpler: the man was still living in Idaho. I located him by phoning long-distance and asking for directory assistance.

When I identified myself, Arnold replied, "I'm pretty fed up with reporters." He said that people from his regional paper, the *Idaho Daily Statesman*, had been seeking an interview for years. In one instance when a reporter telephoned: "I listened to his reasons and then I quietly hung up."

Afraid of exactly that response, I eased into the conversation. I said that I was not only a writer but an aviation enthusiast (which was true, I'd worked as an aircraft mechanic in the Air Force), so for a few moments we talked aviation before drifting back to the original subject. In the process, I must have conveyed some small knowledge of the UFO phenomenon, for Arnold said abruptly: "You seem to understand this [UFO] business pretty well; did you by chance read my book? Most reporters have never even looked at it, which is part of the reason I won't talk to them. They don't know a damn thing other than that I saw flying saucers."

At this point I explained that I had in fact read his book, and that I was familiar with the essential details but would be only too happy to hear more.

"Well, if you've read the book, you have most of the details," Arnold replied. "You know, the quotes in the book are not made up like a lot of people believe. At the time I owned one of the very early [tape] recorders, and I carried it with me to Tacoma."

Ken Arnold's sighting near Mount Rainier not only made him an inviting target for the press but also

caused him to be inundated with mail. There were so
many letters, he said, that "I just couldn't answer
them all."

The experience, meanwhile, had prompted him
to file a report with the commanding officer at
Wright Field, Dayton, Ohio (today Wright-Patterson
AFB). Also, at about this time, he was contacted by
Ray Palmer, who asked Arnold to consider writing a
magazine article about his Mount Rainier sighting.
Arnold declined to write the article, instead sending
Palmer a copy of his report to the Air Force.

A few days later Palmer wrote back, telling
Arnold about a letter he had received from a harbor
patrol officer near Tacoma, Washington. According
to Palmer, the writer of the letter claimed that he and
another man had spotted flying discs over Maury
Island, a small peninsula located about three miles
north of Tacoma Harbor in Puget Sound. The writer
further claimed that one of the discs had dropped
metallic fragments onto the island. Palmer wanted
Arnold to fly to Tacoma and investigate the story, all
expenses paid.

Shortly thereafter, Arnold was visited by Lieutenant Frank Brown and Captain William Davidson,
representatives of A–2 Military Intelligence of the
Fourth (Army) Air Force. They had been assigned the
task of investigating the UFO phenomenon. They
questioned Arnold on all aspects of his sighting and
then, with the pilot's permission, examined his mail.
At the end of their visit the two officers left a telephone number so Arnold could contact them if the
need arose.

Several days later, Arnold decided to accept
Palmer's offer to investigate the Maury Island incident. He taxied his single engine aircraft to the end

of a pasture near his home and throttled forward into what he later called "the doggonedest mystery a man could ever dream of."

On the evening of July 29, 1947, he landed at Berry Field, a small airstrip just outside Tacoma where he felt sure no one would recognize him (his picture had been splashed all over the newspapers). When he tried to make hotel reservations via the airfield's telephone, he discovered that every facility was booked and the city was in the throes of a housing shortage.

In a last and seemingly futile attempt he telephoned the Winthrop Hotel, the largest and most expensive in the city. He was shocked to learn that a room had been reserved in his name! Only two people knew that Arnold was planning a trip to Tacoma: his wife and Ray Palmer. Neither of them had reserved the room. In fact, Arnold had not even bothered to file a flight plan. He felt certain the hotel clerk was confusing him with another Ken Arnold, but he decided to accept the room, feeling equally certain he'd never find another anywhere in the city.

After settling into the hotel, Arnold checked the local telephone directory and found a listing for Harold Dahl, one of the two harbor patrolmen identified by Ray Palmer. On phoning Dahl, the pilot discovered that the man was reluctant to discuss his sighting. In fact, Dahl rather pointedly told Arnold to forget the matter and go home, but Arnold was persistent and finally convinced the man to stop by the hotel room for an interview. Dahl showed up that same evening, and after a bit of prodding, told his story.

On the afternoon of June 21, 1947, he had been operating his boat off Maury Island, accompanied by his son, two crewmen, and the family dog. Suddenly

Dahl spotted six "doughnut-shaped" objects flying overhead at an altitude of about two thousand feet. One of the objects appeared to be in trouble as it was gradually losing altitude. It began discharging lava-like material from its underside—material that fell in large quantities on both the boat and the beach at Maury Island. A fragment, Dahl said, hit his son, causing injury to the boy's arm. Another struck and killed the dog. The boat itself was substantially damaged. Following this, all six discs gained altitude and moved off toward the open sea.

According to Dahl, about twenty tons of hot, slag-like material had been dumped onto the beach. After the substance cooled somewhat, the men collected a large quantity of samples and returned to the mainland, where Dahl's boy was hospitalized.

The incident was related to Dahl's superior, Fred Lee Crisman, who at first didn't believe the story, Dahl said. It was Crisman, however, who had sent the letter to Ray Palmer.

The next morning, June 22, Dahl said he was visited by a stranger wearing a black suit and driving a 1947 Buick. The visitor invited Dahl downtown for breakfast. Dahl accepted, thinking the man was a customer for his part-time salvage operation. Inside a cafe, the stranger related the entire sequence of events occurring off Maury Island. He also told Dahl that it would not be wise to discuss the incident if he wished his family to remain healthy. Strangely, Dahl failed to heed the advice, claiming he immediately drove to the docks where he told fellow workers of this latest episode.

On the morning after his interview with Dahl, Arnold received a visit from both Dahl and Fred Crisman.

Crisman related what he knew of Dahl's story, adding that when he first heard the tale he was convinced the man was lying to explain away the damage to the boat. However, he finally visited Maury Island where he not only found the slag material but also saw one of the doughnut discs cruising overhead.

When Dahl and Crisman departed, Arnold telephoned Captain E. J. Smith, a United Airlines pilot who had also spotted UFOs.[3] Arnold was beginning to suspect he was out of his depth with the investigation and he said as much to Smith. He asked for help. The airline pilot agreed, and Arnold subsequently flew to Seattle to rendezvous with his friend. From then on, events got even stranger.

Every conversation in Arnold's room was monitored by an unseen agency and telephoned verbatim to reporters in the city. The pilots learned of the leak from Ted Morillo, a United Press reporter, who said a mystery informant was phoning in their conversations. The men tore the hotel room apart looking for bugging devices, but found none.

At first, Arnold denied the accuracy of the leaked information. Later, however, he admitted to Morillo that the details were on target. Along with Smith, he began to suspect that either Crisman or Dahl was the source of the leak. But the pilots soon discovered that the phone calls were being made even while the harbor patrolmen were in the room with them. Finally, in desperation, Arnold telephoned the two Army intelligence officers, Lieutenant Brown and Captain Davidson. They arrived the same day, listened to Crisman's recollection of both his and Dahl's alleged sightings, and then suddenly decided they had to leave! (Dahl was not present. He fled the room when he learned the military was being called in.)

"We practically begged them [the Army officers] to stay," Arnold observed during the interview. "But they claimed they had to get their plane to some air show the next day."

The officers departed, carrying slag samples given to them by Crisman. That same night the military plane transporting Brown and Davidson crashed, killing both men. The flight chief and one other person aboard, an Army enlisted man, parachuted to safety.

On the morning of August 1, 1947, the story of the wrecked transport appeared in banner headlines in the *Tacoma Times*. The story revealed the names of the two Army officers even before the military officially identified them! The story was by a *Times* staff writer, Paul Lance. His source of information, he later told Arnold and Smith, was the anonymous telephone caller.

Two weeks after the story broke, Paul Lance died unexpectedly. "Maybe it was coincidence," Arnold said.

Ted Morillo, the United Press reporter, subsequently lost his job and suffered numerous personal difficulties. A persistent newsman, he had employed his own network of informants in an effort to trace the identity of the mystery caller. He never succeeded. He finally suggested to Smith and Arnold that they leave town for their own safety.

Crisman disappeared and it was rumored (by the anonymous caller again) that he had departed Tacoma aboard an Alaska-bound military transport. Dahl was found sitting in a movie theater and, according to Arnold, seemed unconcerned about the deaths of the two Army intelligence men.

Arnold himself nearly suffered a fate similar to that of the two Army officers. En route home he stopped for fuel. On takeoff, the aircraft engine stalled, and only quick thinking and skilled piloting saved him from a fatal crash.

Following the incident at Tacoma, Ken Arnold grew resentful and angry over what he believed was an inappropriate response to UFO sightings on the part of the government. He said a sense of loyalty had prompted him to file a report on the flying discs—he believed they were a new type of foreign aircraft spying on his country. But instead of being congratulated, he, Smith, and other pilots were all "made to look like Goddamn jerks."

Both Arnold and Smith continued to fly in the years afterward, Smith commercially and Arnold as a private flier. Of his friend Smith, Arnold said, "He retired after thirty-eight years at the age of sixty. They had a banquet in his honor but I couldn't attend."

In 1949 or 1950, Arnold turned down a fifty thousand dollar offer from Doubleday for the rights to his story—a tremendous sum from any publisher at the time. "They wanted to have someone ghost-write the book," Arnold said. "I wanted it in my own words, so I turned down their offer." Film rights too remained with Arnold due to the flier's insistence that the story be documented accurately. In the end, the only complete account of the incident came from Arnold's collaboration with Ray Palmer, first as an article in *Fate* and later as the book *The Coming of the Saucers*. There was, however, another written account—one never intended for public consumption.

Amid rumors of sabotage and espionage in connection with the crash of the military transport, the

FBI initiated a field investigation that included interviews with the various Maury Island players. The result was a fifteen-page report to the director compiled by Jack B. Wilcox, special agent in charge, in Seattle. The report was dated August 18, 1947.

A copy of the report, made available under the Freedom of Information Act, remained heavily censored even after nearly fifty years, particularly in the matter of names. However, because the chief players were already known through Arnold's account and subsequent stories, it was a simple matter to fit an appropriate name to most blanks.

Judging by the report, the FBI quickly concluded that the Maury Island episode was a hoax. If my placement of names in the censored document is at all accurate, it's evident that Dahl and Crisman were suspect almost from the start.

One section of the report, for instance, describes a news interview with Harold Dahl at the subject's home. According to the account, the reporter was attempting to confirm a story about a "disintegrated" disc near Maury Island. However, during the interview, Dahl's wife reportedly went into a "considerable rage" and demanded that her husband admit the story was a fantasy. The interviewer said Dahl then recanted, acknowledging the flying disc story was a hoax.

During an interview with Dahl and Crisman on August 7, 1947, at the bureau office in Tacoma, the resident FBI agent found the two to be vague and evasive in response to questions. The agent said both men initially "denied making any statement to anyone" suggesting that the slag samples came from a flying disc. It was apparent, the agent continued, that the two men "were not telling their complete and true connection with the flying disc story. They refused to give any definite information ... but gave evasive answers and repeatedly stated that they had nothing to do with it ..."

Faced with a lengthy interrogation, Crisman and Dahl finally told the FBI agent that, in communicating with Ray Palmer, they had manufactured a portion of the flying disc story only because it appeared that "that's what he [Palmer] wanted them to say." The FBI interviewer, however, remained unimpressed with what seemed a total and deliberate fabrication, and in his summary reiterated that "no definite information could be obtained ... as to what each [man] specifically had done to start the flying disc story."

On the matter of the crashed military transport (actually a B–25 bomber), the FBI checked with Fourth Army Air Force investigators at McChord Field, Washington. The bureau was told that an Army investigation had uncovered no hint of sabotage linked to the crash. Indeed the cause of the crash was traced to a faulty exhaust stack that sparked a fire on the left wing. The wing sheared away and in the process tore off the aircraft tail. Rumors (spread by the anonymous caller) that the crash was caused by a bomb or by enemy aircraft gunfire were determined to be as false as the flying discs over Maury Island.

(A point here concerns the sudden departure of the Army investigators following their interview with Fred Crisman. The two, Brown and Davidson, must have observed some detail in Crisman's story that gave away the hoax. If so, none of this was conveyed to Ken Arnold, probably because the two officers were under orders to remain silent about anything they discovered.)

Murkier was the identity of the anonymous caller who, among other things, tipped reporters to the identities of Brown and Davidson even before the Army had released the names of the two men. Five anonymous calls were made to various newspaper offices between 11:30 A.M. on July 31, and 5:30 P.M. on August 2, 1947. The FBI clearly suspected Crisman of being responsible for the calls in some way. Even so, the bureau never succeeded in tracing the identity of the caller.

The "fragments" from Maury Island were another matter entirely. Bureau investigators quickly found that they bore a "distinct resemblance" to slag from a smelter near Tacoma. What's more, there is nothing in the FBI report to suggest that the slag was radioactive—something mentioned by others who have attempted to review this episode.

Once it became apparent that the flying disc story was a sham and (at least officially) that the crash of the Army aircraft was an accident and not sabotage, the FBI closed its files on Maury Island.

Some final notes on the principal players:

Fred Crisman never went to Alaska despite rumors to that effect. Instead, according to journalist John Keel,[4] he was caught up in the war in Korea and later became a public school teacher. Crisman eventually adopted the identity of Jon Gold, a radio talk show host in Tacoma. In 1968, he was summoned to New Orleans by District Attorney Jim Garrison, who was conducting an inquiry into the Kennedy assassination. Crisman was tenuously linked to the assassination through photos taken at the time in Dallas—one of which showed a man who looked like Crisman.

Keel reported that someone tried to kill Crisman just before his summons to New Orleans. The attempt had nothing to do with the death of Kennedy and much to do with Crisman's abrasive radio presence; he had, evidently, antagonized a good many people with his wit and aggressive personality.

Crisman died of natural causes in 1975, leaving ufologists and Kennedy conspiracy theorists to continue to puzzle over the man's past. Many felt he had ties to the intelligence community, particularly the CIA, although the reasoning behind this is as tenuous as his supposed presence in Dallas. On the other hand, Crisman's ability to confound the FBI in Tacoma in 1947, plus his possible connection to the anonymous telephone caller, leaves one to wonder if there isn't some truth in this view.

Crisman's cohort, Harold Dahl, moved to a different address soon after the incident. Meanwhile, his teenaged son disappeared, only to turn up in another state suffering, reportedly, from amnesia. Others have written that young Dahl was found by authorities in Colorado or Wyoming. According to the FBI account, the father said the boy turned up in Montana. There was no mention that the youth suffered from amnesia, simply that he had run away.

Dahl, incidentally, was not and had never been a harbor patrol officer. This was a persona he and Crisman adopted for the sake of their story, although the two did own and operate a supply boat in Tacoma harbor.

Publisher Ray Palmer, who was clearly duped by Crisman into pursuing the Maury Island story, spent his final years in relative obscurity. His death in 1977 brought an end to an era in UFO reporting— silencing what was once perhaps the strongest voice in the field.

18

Kenneth Arnold lived on for many active years before his death on January 16, 1984, in a hospital in Bellevue, Washington. Despite his Mount Rainier sighting and his unwanted fame, he never thought of himself as anyone special—maintaining all along that he was "just an ordinary sort of guy."

NOTES
1. Under the National Security Act of 1947, the Army Air Corps became the Air Force on September 18 of that year. Initiated by President Truman, this action was opposed by Navy leaders who feared they would lose control of maritime aviation.
2. Curt Sutherly, "Ken Arnold—First American Pilot to Report UFOs," *Saga's UFO Report*, March, 1977, pp. 42–43, 62, 64–65, 70.
3. Nine flying discs were spotted by Smith and a co-pilot, Ralph Stevens, on July 4, 1947, just after the two had taken off from the Boise, Idaho, airport. Their description of the discs was similar to Arnold's, but the July 4 objects flew in two groups of four and five each.
4. John A. Keel, "The Maury Island Caper," *UFOs: 1947–1987*, compiled and edited by Hilary Evans with John Spencer for the British UFO Research Association (1987), pp. 40–43.

Chapter Two:

The Invasion of Boshkung Lake

It all began the evening of November 23, 1973. Canadian realtors Earl Pitts and Jim Cooper were driving on Route 35 to their homes near Boshkung Lake in the town of Minden, Ontario. Suddenly an "awesome thing," as Pitts later described it, flashed through the sky from west to east and vanished from sight in seconds. The object, which the men estimated to be eighteen feet long, was "large in front and tapered" with a glowing front end and a white light at the tail.

Private pilot Dale Parnell of Stormy Lake, driving home that night with his wife, watched another (or perhaps the same) object pass nearby on Buckhorn Road. Pete Sawyer, of Hall's Lake, also spotted a strange flying object, though his sighting was during daylight hours. He told reporters that it looked like a helicopter without a tail. "It came down the gully by Shaws' heading for Boshkung Lake," he said. The top of the object was illuminated, the bottom half dark, and "that was the last I saw of it." Sawyer added that the object had four legs or landing gear that appeared to be partly raised.

Three months later, weird flying objects were still hanging around Boshkung Lake. Mr. and Mrs. Ashley Lunham, residing in a lakeside house, told reporter Peter Courtney of the *Minden Progress* that strange aerial objects had scarcely missed a night since mid-November. The UFOs made no overt attempt to disturb residents or interfere with them, Mrs. Lunham said. But she did recall one rather disquieting incident.

The couple had just finished dinner one afternoon during mid-February 1974, when they saw a UFO move over the lake and turn toward their house. Midway across the lake the object began to glow with a brilliant white light as if generating excessive energy. The burst of power lasted for only a second or two, but in that brief interval the frost on the Lunhams' dining room windows *melted!* When Mrs. Lunham went to wipe up the water she discovered the glass was so hot "I couldn't touch it." The outside temperature at that time was twenty degrees below zero.

The Boshkung Lake UFOs arrived in assorted shapes and colors. Some objects were cigar-shaped and some were "polliwog" shaped. Some flashed amber, red, blue, or white lights. Others were rust-brown or black in color, or sometimes a dull red. Each was reported to be carrying up to nine external "antennae," though they seemed to communicate, not by radio, but by flashing a kind of code back and forth with bright lights.

According to the Lunhams, flying objects appeared over the lake nearly every evening at sundown throughout the winter, arriving first singly or in pairs,

22

then in greater numbers until the frozen lake surface was a virtual parking lot. The objects would then either settle to the surface, hang stationary over nearby power lines (a common UFO practice), or hover above holes in the ice that remained after ice fishermen had moved their huts. The UFO occupants, if there were any, were never seen.

After weeks of this nightly activity, the Lunhams decided to call the authorities. They may as well not have bothered. An officer of the Ontario Provincial Police arrived on the scene, pronounced the objects "reflections," and departed. After he had gone, the "reflections" shot straight up into the sky and streaked above the lake, their light reflected in its frozen surface.

The Lunhams next tried to interest the Canadian Department of National Defense. There they met with even less success.

On the morning of February 26, 1974, four UFOs were spotted within forty feet of the Lunhams' home. These objects were of a different shape and design than any they'd seen before. Each had four wings, and an overall wingspan of about twenty feet. They were dark in color, and equipped with blue-white lights. Each, as it abruptly departed, discharged a fog.

Taken as a whole, the objects over Boshkung Lake were an unworldly conglomerate. They looked nothing at all like conventional aircraft. Their manner of flight was strange: takeoff was described as an upward bouncing motion not unlike a rubber ball. Sometimes when they launched they made an audible sound, a kind of dull "thumping" that faded as soon as the UFO was airborne. In flight horizontally, they moved erratically, and at greatly varying speeds.

Mrs. Lunham told reporters she didn't believe the objects were from outer space because they appeared almost every night for months. What's more, she said the UFO power plants didn't seem highly advanced—subject, evidently, to the same sort of problems as earthly engines: "Sometimes they start to fail ..." She said a UFO experienced difficulty starting up the morning of Tuesday, February 26.

On Sunday, March 10, 1974, journalist Peter Courtney spotted a UFO over Boshkung Lake. The sighting—his first after a number of visits—was described in a *Minden Progress* article dated March 14.

In the article, Courtney acknowledged that one of his assignments was to cover the recurring UFO activity in Haliburton County, and in particular the Boshkung Lake area. After four trips he had collected numerous accounts, but he personally had observed nothing unusual. Then came the fifth trip. Wearing a snowmobile suit, and equipped with a 35-mm camera and tripod for night photography, he arrived at the lake's east shore. The time, he reported in his article, was about 9:00 P.M. The weather was mild and the sky cloudless. The entire lake, he said, was "bathed in bright moonlight."

An hour passed and Courtney had about decided that this was to be another uneventful trip when "a dull red light" appeared on the far side of the lake. Moving above the treetops, the light traveled north in a slow, erratic manner before retracing its path and flying out of sight. The newsman had his camera ready, but the glowing red light proved too dull to photograph. Its movements, he wrote, were "too erratic" to be those of a regular aircraft, and he admitted that he was at a loss to explain away the object. He concluded that it "defied rational explanation."

While Courtney was quietly watching and puzzling over the strange flying light, others were preparing an ambush. That night more than fifty people gathered elsewhere along the lake shore, determined to do something—anything—about the aerial interlopers. At about 10:00 P.M., the time of Courtney's sighting, members of a six-unit snowmobile squad took to the ice, firing high-powered rifles at the approaching UFOs. Mrs. Lunham told reporters that "a distant clunk" could be heard as bullets struck the exterior of the flying objects. Her reaction was nervousness and uneasiness. "I've had about as much of this as I can take," she said.

She wasn't the only resident fed up with the weird goings-on: Mrs. William Barnes, a housewife who—along with her husband—had watched UFOs near their home in Lochlin, Ontario, told reporters that a number of people had seen the objects and no one knew what to make of them. "We can't all be crazy," she observed.

One evening at the end of March 1974, Mr. and Mrs. Barnes watched a UFO maneuver about a half-mile from their house. Like many of the objects appearing over the lake, it sported red, white, and blue lights. Two nights later the same—or a very similar—UFO returned to the exact location, but this time was joined by a second object. Mr. and Mrs. Barnes and a neighbor, Mrs. Lester Hicks, reported that the objects hovered for a time; then one of the two flew off rapidly. The second UFO departed more slowly, at a "cruising" speed, until it abruptly—and amazingly—dropped to the ground "out of sight!"

As the UFO sightings continued, residents of the area began finding what they believed were landing traces. Sometimes the trace was little more than a "depression" in the heavy lake ice. Other times it was significant, such as an odd pattern in the snow discovered by the Lunhams not far from their house. The unusual pattern was shown to *Lindsay* (Ontario) *Post* reporters, who described it in a March 14, 1974 story.

According to the *Post*, the pattern formed a "V-shape" in the snow combined with two "pad-like" markings. It was located within a copse of trees and was clearly visible despite erosion caused by the warm March sunshine. However, the pattern was only slightly odder than the location itself—within a wooded area. The *Post* observed that if the copse had sheltered a flying craft (and this was by no means certain), then the craft was either small enough to penetrate the trees, or it had dropped to earth else-where and maneuvered to the location behind the Lunham house.

UFO activity at the lake continued well into April 1974. The final sighting of any consequence took place during the middle of the month, when Mrs. Wallace Brown of Lochlin looked out her bay window and observed an object with blue, green, and yellow lights moving erratically through the sky. Her television set became inoperative while the object was in the area. Neighbors also reported electromagnetic effects while the UFO was in the vicinity.

What all of this means is anyone's guess. However, as Mrs. Lunham observed, the objects at Boshkung Lake were probably not craft from outer space. Too many questions are raised by their long-term presence and activity—questions which fail to satisfy an extraterrestrial explanation.

If the objects were in fact spacecraft, they were powered by amazingly primitive engines—engines no better than terrestrial machines, starting with difficulty on cold winter mornings. Also, there is this business of objects dropping to the ground out of sight: vanishing, apparently, into the very earth. Finally, there are the sheer numbers of objects to be considered, and the fact that not once did anyone see occupants!

Mysterious, peculiar, and even a trifle absurd, the Boshkung Lake UFOs—like their innumerable counterparts spotted around the world—appear destined to remain a mystery for a very long time to come.

Chapter Three:

Black Squares and
Electric Railroad Lanterns

The cold was numbing, the temperature near zero, when the "thing" arrived and buried itself in the mud and silt at the bottom of William McCarthy's farm pond. The event rippled through the sleepy town of Wakefield (pop. 1,400), interrupting a New Year that, although cold and snowy, was otherwise unremarkable.

Located in southeast New Hampshire not far from the Maine border, Wakefield was understandably unprepared for its mysterious visitor. The day was January 10, 1977. Thomas McCarthy, twenty-six, found himself out in the cold, staring at the frozen surface of his father's pond where something very odd was occurring. The entire pond was beginning to melt and "it was five degrees above zero" with a blizzard in progress, he later explained.

Startled and a bit shaken, Thomas alerted his parents, William and Dorothy, to the melting ice. They soon found that the one hundred-foot-long pond contained a hole in the frozen surface some three feet in diameter and perfectly round. What's more, "a black square object" could be seen through the hole, settling into the pond bottom.

The strange black object had penetrated ice that was eighteen inches thick, fifty-two-year-old William McCarthy later told reporters. He said he had no "logical explanation" for what had occurred except that perhaps a piece of space hardware from a "disintegrating space capsule or booster" had struck his pond.

McCarthy, a professional breeder of saddle horses, gave a more detailed account of his observations to UFO researcher Betty Hill of Portsmouth, New Hampshire. Hill passed along the information in a letter dated January 29, 1977. She wrote: "McCarthy told me that he found the eighteen-inch-thick ice melting, and it continued to melt while he watched. He looked down into the hole and saw a twelve-inch-square black object, which was also seen by two other family members [wife Dorothy, and son Thomas]."

Curiosity overwhelming his better judgment, McCarthy decided to try to retrieve the object. "He went to the barn for a hoe, rake, and a long stick." Using the stick as a probe, McCarthy discovered "that the object had apparently settled into the mud at the bottom of the pond, for he found a three-foot hole [in the mud] the same shape as the object." By now, according to Hill, McCarthy had begun to feel "very uncomfortable" due to the storm and extremely cold temperature.

Returning to the house, McCarthy notified a friend who in turn contacted police. The call for assistance, as it turned out, proved to be about the same as opening a Pandora's Box.

Two police officers arrived soon thereafter with a Geiger counter and checked the pond for radiation. According to Betty Hill, they got a reading of about four roentgens—high enough to be considered potentially dangerous and prompting a warning that the family should not allow the horses to drink from the pond. (For purposes of comparison, radioactive fallout from a distant nuclear test is usually measured in thousandths of a roentgen.) Soon Civil Defense (CD) personnel arrived and took additional readings. In a statement to reporters, George McAvoy, then director of Civil Defense for New Hampshire observed: "It's not a hoax. There was some phenomenon."

CD Deputy Director Wesley Williams, who took the first Civil Defense readings, told the media that three different counters showed three different readings. One Geiger counter read zero, one low, and one about three roentgens per hour. Williams said that when he arrived the pond ice was still melting, so he was forced to take his readings at a distance of several yards from a marker indicating the original three-foot hole. He noted that he was in over his boots while still ten feet from the marker. The instrument that gave a high reading was later returned to a Civil Defense laboratory for suspected equipment failure. According to George McAvoy, no amount of testing revealed any fault with the counter. Subsequent testing of the other two instruments also uncovered no problem.

Twelve hours after the first readings were taken, Geiger counters showed negative radioactivity around the pond. However, federal officials (Energy Research and Development Administration, Washington, D.C.) speculated that if an object had indeed settled to the bottom, the combination of water, ice, and mud might have blocked further radiation emissions, making them undetectable.

In the days following the arrival of the "thing," as it came to be known, the Wakefield Pandora's Box opened still further, allowing the demons of bureaucracy to spill out onto the countryside.

On Thursday, January 13, 1977, state officials arrived, examined the pond, and decided there was nothing hidden beneath the ice and mud. Included in this task force were members of the National Guard, representatives of the New Hampshire Disaster Office, assorted health officials, and individuals from the state's Criminal Division. The task force placed the area under tight security, and everyone in town was told not to talk about the thing that wasn't there.

Meanwhile, the office of New Hampshire Governor Meldrim Thomson, Jr. was explaining how "the entire report is false; [there is] no evidence of any foreign object in the small pond." At about the same time, WBZ–TV in Boston was airing a film clip showing a basketball-sized mass being removed from the pond (later said to have been mud and silt samples from the pond floor).

As if this weren't enough, Colonel Leon Parker of the state adjutant's office put his foot in his mouth when he contradicted Governor Thomson: "We know some object dropped into the farmer's pond," he stated publicly.

At about the same time, a Pentagon spokesperson in Washington, D.C. told reporters that New Hampshire National Guard officials wanted to know if the object was a fallen artificial satellite. An inquiry to the North American Air Defense Command (ADC) had been made by the Guard, but according to the spokesperson, an ADC check showed no evidence that a satellite—or any part of one—had fallen on Wakefield.

In Wakefield itself, speculation abounded despite the official "gag order." According to William McCarthy, the attitude in the town was that if you were not supposed to talk about it, then "there must be something to it." The farmer admitted to reporters that he had been swamped with telephone calls from excited individuals: "What color are the spaceships?" one caller asked. McCarthy, calm despite the unrest around him, said such calls were an exaggeration. There were no "little green men," he said, and no "flashing lights," and no "thunder."

Meanwhile, the Wakefield "thing" was news even in Canada. On January 13, 1977, television stations in Ontario reported that an odd tremor had rattled the town of Cobourg (pop. 11,000). What made the tremor unusual, the media reported, was that it not only happened just before the "crash" in Wakefield, but it also failed to register on seismic instruments.

Some observers noted that Cobourg is only a few miles from Port Hope, Ontario, where nuclear research was being conducted. That Cobourg should be shaken as Wakefield received a radioactive object from the sky seemed like an odd sort of coincidence. Furthermore, Wakefield and Cobourg are not far apart geographically: separated in a straight line by no more than four hundred miles. Still, it is unlikely that the Wakefield object was linked in any way to research at Port Hope. On the other hand, it is possible that the shock wave felt in Cobourg was caused by the object, which may have been moving faster than sound before hitting the pond. The object would have left an audible track (a sonic boom) along a path that may have taken it over Cobourg. This, however, raises another question: Why was there no shock wave or audible disturbance at the point of impact? One answer is that the object, device, whatever it was (and keep in mind its reported shape), slowed down before hitting the pond! It came in under controlled flight.

Strange objects have a way of falling into small lakes and ponds. Three years earlier, on November 9, 1974, in the town of Carbondale, Pennsylvania, a "mysterious glowing object" plunged into a small silt pond on the outskirts of the town. There, as in Wakefield, officials did their best to shroud the incident in secrecy while insisting that the affair was nothing more than a hoax.

The Carbondale "fireball," as it came to be known, was spotted at about 7:00 P.M. on November 9 by three teenage boys: Bill Lloyd, his younger brother, John, and a friend, Bob Gillette. The boys told Carbondale police that when they first saw the object, it looked like a red fireball. They said it approached from the east, crossed over nearby Salem Mountain and then hovered! An instant later it plunged into the pond. According to the three youngsters, the UFO "turned the color of a bright star" while it hovered. Police later admitted they received at least one earlier phone call about a UFO.

Within the hour other calls came into police headquarters. Finally, around 9:00 P.M., officers John Barbaro and Joseph Jacobina were dispatched to the pond where they reported seeing a "glowing object" about twenty feet out in the water. Shortly thereafter, acting police chief Francis Dottle was notified;

he dispatched twelve additional (regular and special) police to the scene. Officers also arrived from nearby Forest City, and from Greenfield and Fell townships. At one point, officer Jacobina discharged his service revolver into the water and, according to Bob Gillette, the glow "moved." No further action was taken until after midnight, when fire fighters arrived from a nearby community armed with a huge net.

According to a report published in the *Scranton* (Pennsylvania) *Times*, the scene around the pond took on "the look of a science fiction thriller as the net was hooked around the object." This was at about 2:45 A.M. As the fire fighters hauled on the net, the glowing object slipped free and settled into the silt at the bottom of the pond. Later the glow vanished, and police surmised that the object had become buried under the silt. No additional attempts to raise the light were made that night.

Sunday, November 10, two professors from Philadelphia's Temple University arrived and asked permission to don scuba gear and search the pond bottom. The two were Dr. Laurence Berry, a psychologist, and George Kelly, a meteorology instructor. However, Chief Dottle would not allow the men to dive. Next, police contacted Dr. J. Allen Hynek, then head of the Center for UFO Studies in Illinois. Hynek informed police that a UFO investigator from Port Crane, New York, would be dispatched to act as an advisor. Events as they occurred from this point on are unclear—the details mired in confusion and obscurity.

At the time of the Carbondale "fireball," I was just learning how to work seriously at my writing. Up until then I had been penning stories and news articles on a part-time basis while holding down various "normal" jobs. Now I was taking the plunge as a full-time free-lance writer. My new routine included serving as a regular correspondent for the *Daily News* in Lebanon County, some three hours drive time from Carbon-dale. Rob McNamee, the newspaper's city editor, assigned me to the "fireball" story and sent me on my way. However, by the time I arrived in Carbondale, the entire episode had been branded a hoax, with the Lloyd brothers and Gillette made to look like pranksters.

When I approached Chief Dottle, explaining my reason for being there, the man stared for a moment then shouted, "Not another one! This town's been crawling with reporters." A silence followed as I tried to decide how best to deal with the man. Dot-tle himself broke the silence as he reached behind his desk and waved a silvery object in my face. "This is your UFO!" he declared. It was an electric rail-road lantern.

Surprised, but suspicious, I continued to press for details about the events of the two previous days. Between terse, impatient answers, Dottle managed to make one point especially clear: he wanted me to leave Carbondale immediately. The man was clearly frustrated and showing evident stress. Nonetheless, I almost had to smile, as his reaction brought to mind all the old western films I'd ever seen in which the sheriff insisted that the stranger get out of town.

Of course I didn't leave right off. Instead, I spoke with people on the streets and in various places of business, trying to make sense of what had tran-spired during the hours I had been en route. Public attitude was about the same as in Wakefield. Many were convinced that something unknown had fallen into the pond—that the electric lantern was merely a device of convenience, and that local police were reciting a script prepared by higher authority. There was even an unconfirmed report that an object had been taken from the pond, loaded into an unmarked van, and driven away.

Putting aside any and all speculation about origin, as well as the usual "official" pronouncements that there is never anything to it, the fact remains that mysterious objects do drop from the skies, and not always with quiet consideration. On occasion, these aerial visitors raise pure hell.

Such an event occurred at Upper Scott Lake near Pullman, Michigan, just fifteen minutes after the year 1970 began. The lake, located on a YMCA camp ground, was under the supervision of Mr. and Mrs. James Eastep, who were in the camp house playing cards with relatives at the time of the incident.

Suddenly the building shook violently, nearly tossing the card players to the floor. Storm windows blew out of the walls. A mile and a half away, in Pullman, shock waves were felt. Even more astonishing were subsequent reports from the town of Bravo, four miles to the north, where books were thrown from shelves and windows rattled.

Later in the day, Jim Eastep discovered additional damage to the camp. In the dining lodge, picture windows were shattered. So were small window panes and a light fixture, and even the fireplace frame. Wooden window shutters on several cabins also showed heavy damage, looking as if "an ax had cut them to ribbons."

When he searched beyond the buildings, the caretaker discovered a huge hole—forty feet across—

in the icy lake surface. The hole was about two hundred yards from shore. Ice chunks thrown from the lake were scattered as much as one hundred feet from the hole, which appeared to be the point of impact of something from above.

Sheriff's deputies called to the scene decided that, probably because it was New Year's Day, somebody had been playing with dynamite. Persons experienced in the use of heavy explosives were quick to ridicule this theory, noting that an incredible amount of TNT would be needed to cause such damage (not to mention sending the shock waves four miles). Eastep himself said he had witnessed a truck load of dynamite explode in Korea in the same type of weather, and that blast caused less noise and shock.

Still other puzzling factors came to light. One resident claimed that, just before the explosion, he heard the sound of an aircraft passing over the camp. Another individual said the needle of her home barometer started whirling prior to the blast. Moreover, there was the strange mound of mud found by Eastep and his brother-in-law, Dale Lamb. This mound, containing seaweed from the lake bed, had oozed upward through a three-foot hole in the ice about thirty-five feet from shore, forming a bulge two feet high. By afternoon on New Year's Day, the mound had receded. Clearly something struck the lake; something with highly unusual and potentially deadly properties.

On January 16, 1977, the *Boston Globe* published an editorial entitled "The Wakefield Monster," which effectively capsulized both private and official attitudes regarding events in that town. In part, it appeared as follows (reprinted courtesy of the *Boston Globe*):

> Four days of speculation, inspection, tests and jabs at the pond have left the tiny town on the Maine border with little more than an argument over whether anything out of the ordinary ever happened at all.
>
> Witnesses to the "alleged" event, as newspapers are calling the activity, claim that on Monday a 3-foot-wide hole appeared in the 18-inch-thick ice on a farm pond owned by Mr. and Mrs. William McCarthy. Ice around the hole melted, a flat, black object was seen nestled in the mud, more holes developed, and the Wakefield police were summoned.
>
> Wild radioactivity levels were recorded at the site, security was thrown up around the farm, and the New Hampshire National Guard was ordered to search the suspect pond. Spectators at that operation reported that the guardsmen chopped out a big chunk of ice, raised the alleged object and dispatched it to Concord.
>
> There Gov. Meldrim Thomson, Jr., whose response to all of this has included ingeniously ordering the 1,400-odd townspeople into silence, announced after the probe-and-remove mission that nothing had been found and that the alleged mystery was officially over.

Over for whom? For those who may have found something in the pond, doubtlessly! But for the people of Wakefield, and for those who followed the matter from afar with great interest, the mystery—after all these years—remains far from finished.

Are we being protected from some knowledge that military and political leaders feel could cause us harm? Or are we merely being shielded from the fear they themselves know every time they deal with the unknown?

Chapter Four:

The Disinformation Game

There are those who believe the United States Government, quite literally, has the answer to the UFO puzzle. They claim that on a stormy night in July 1947, an alien spacecraft crashed in an arid region of New Mexico, and that military personnel retrieved both wreckage and the bodies of the dead crew members.

The story is an old one, circulating for forty years as nothing more than a rumor. In 1987, a new twist was added: a mysterious document that stated the crash had prompted a top-secret government operation. At last, there seemed to be proof.

A storm of controversy quickly ensued. Accusations and demands were rife within UFO research groups. The debate found its way into print and even onto television. UFO buffs everywhere came to know the code name for the government operation supposedly behind it all: "Majestic 12" or MJ–12.

In mid-1989, I was asked to write a magazine article[5] examining the validity of the MJ–12 document. The editor wanted a comprehensive piece—an article that would include everything then known on the subject. Not long after, I received a copy of the MJ–12 document from Floyd Murray of Folsom, Pennsylvania. Murray, a veteran researcher, also sent photocopies of related papers and articles and, on request, obtained necessary telephone numbers. Sifting through the material took weeks. More time was spent interviewing various persons. Eventually the article was completed.

In the process, I learned that the MJ–12 papers first surfaced in December 1984, when they were sent on undeveloped 35-mm film to Jaime Shandera, a Los Angeles-based documentary film producer. Shandera and two associates, Stanton T. Friedman and William L. Moore, both well-known in UFO research circles, withheld the document until May 1987, ostensibly to try to determine its validity before releasing it to a wider audience.

The legend of the "crashed UFO," which is at the heart of the MJ–12 papers, has been publicized in numerous books and on television programs such as NBC's *Unsolved Mysteries*. Briefly, the story is this:

In early July 1947, a public relations officer at Roswell Army Air Base, New Mexico, issued a statement which said, in part: "... the intelligence office of the 509th [Atomic] Bomb Group of the Eighth Air Force, Roswell Army Air Base, was fortunate enough to gain possession of a disc through the cooperation of one of the local ranchers and the Sheriff's office of Chaves County.... Action was immediately taken and the disc was picked up at the rancher's home. It was inspected at the Roswell Army Air Field and subsequently loaned by Major [Jesse] Marcel [the intelligence officer in charge of the retrieval operation] to higher headquarters."

Almost immediately the story was recanted by higher headquarters. Instead of a flying disc, the object was said to be the "wreckage of a high altitude weather observation device," consisting of a "box-kite and a balloon" along with a "star-shaped tinfoil target to reflect radar." The balloon explanation was attributed to Army Brigadier General Roger M. Ramey, commander of the Eighth Air Force at Fort Worth.[6]

Ramey's explanation notwithstanding, the rumor persisted that the object really was a disc. Forty years later, the MJ–12 papers seemed to verify the story of a crashed alien craft.

Dated November 18, 1952, the MJ–12 document appears to be a briefing written by Rear Admiral R. H. Hillenkoetter for President-elect Dwight D. Eisenhower. Also included is a purported memorandum, dated September 24, 1947, signed by President Harry Truman to Defense Secretary James Forrestal, calling for the creation of "Operation Majestic 12."

Majestic 12, according to page 2 of the briefing document, is "a Top Secret Research and Development/Intelligence operation responsible only to the President of the United States." This alleged operation is carried out at the direction of twelve highly placed individuals having a combined military/civilian background—hence the code name.

"On 07 July, 1947," the document continues, "a secret operation was begun to assure recovery of the wreckage of this object for scientific study." It goes on to state that "four small human-like beings had apparently ejected from the craft at some point before it exploded." The bodies were found some "two miles east of the wreckage site. All four were dead and *badly decomposed* [emphasis added] due to action by predators and exposure to the elements during the approximately one-week time period which had elapsed before their discovery."

I have spoken with naturalists having a working knowledge of animal decomposition, with a veterinarian, and with a coroner of many years experience. All have rendered essentially the same opinion: a body—human or animal—would not "badly decompose" in a hot, dry region. Instead, the arid desert environment would dehydrate the carcass, resulting in a kind of mummification.

Of course, one might suppose the biological makeup of the bodies was so different as to result in rapid decomposition even in the desert. Page 4 of the MJ–12 document contains a statement referring to the alleged alien biology. It reads: "Although these creatures are human-like in appearance, the biological and evolutionary processes responsible for their development has [sic] apparently been quite different from those observed or postulated in homo-sapiens."

If so, then it is doubtful that wild scavengers or predators would have found the meat of the carcasses at all interesting. Indeed, within Earth's own community of creatures there is precedent to uphold this view: the opossum, the only North American marsupial, is almost never bothered by natural predators simply because it is possessed of a somewhat disagreeable odor.[7]

Furthermore, the coroner with whom I spoke noted that if predators or scavengers had attacked the carcasses, they would, after a week, have reduced the bodies to bones.

In short, there is a great deal to suspect about this part of the MJ–12 document. What, then, of the rest of the document?

* * *

When the MJ–12 papers first came to light, two researchers in particular were immediately at odds over whether or not the document is genuine. One is Philip J. Klass. The other is Stanton Friedman. Neither man is exactly what one might call a dunderhead.

Klass, of Washington, D.C., is an aviation expert and a contributing editor for a leading aviation magazine. He is ufology's best known (and, for some, most despised) skeptical investigator, and is convinced the MJ–12 papers are a hoax.

Friedman, on the other hand, was quite vocal in his defense of the purported document. His background is that of nuclear physicist and UFO lecturer. He has worked on numerous classified government projects, including programs to develop nuclear-powered aircraft and nuclear-thrust rockets.[8] He currently lives in New Brunswick, Canada.

For a long while, the debate between the two men was more or less tit for tat—that is, fairly well balanced, without one gaining much of an advantage over the other. The two seemed almost perfect foils for one another, though sharing, perhaps, an unspoken mutual respect—something I suspect neither man would be quick to admit.

Correspondence had also flown between Klass and William Moore, a West Coast researcher who, from the start, was deeply involved in the MJ–12 matter. Through it all, the filmmaker who received the unprocessed roll of film, Jaime Shandera, maintained a low profile.

In the contest over authenticity of the MJ–12 document, Phil Klass finally seemed to gain the upper hand. In a "White Paper"[9] dated October 12, 1989,[10] he asserted that a Smith Corona typewriter introduced "around 1963" was used to type the

MJ–12 Truman memo of September 24, 1947. The memo, in short, was a counterfeit, and Klass said he had the word of a professional document examiner to support his claim.

This was not, however, the first MJ–12 paper to be declared counterfeit. A document called the "Aquarius" paper—the first to surface referring to MJ–12—was reported to be a retyped version of an Air Force Office of Special Investigations (AFOSI) teletype message. This disclosure was made by William Moore during a controversial two-hour talk at the July 1989 MUFON symposium in Las Vegas, but we'll come back to this.

Klass believed the signature on the September 24, 1947, Truman memorandum was taken from an authentic memo to Dr. Vannevar Bush dated October 1, 1947. The authentic signature, he said, was recopied onto the purported September 24 memo, after which it was brushed to eliminate copy lines around the signature and then photocopied a final time. The signatures are identical, said Klass, except for a slight difference in size caused by the photocopying process.

During a telephone conversation, Klass recounted his effort to obtain expert analysis of the September 24 memo, and also related how that task led him to a man who had earlier been consulting with Moore, Friedman, and Shandera.

Klass's initial effort took him to Joe Nickell, of Lexington, Kentucky, whose hobby is the authenticity of documents. Nickell, however, is a member of the executive council of the Committee for the Scientific Investigation of Claims of the Paranormal (CSICOPS)—an organization to which Klass also belongs and which remains at odds with nearly all segments of the UFO community.

Realizing that any opinion by Nickell would be held in great suspicion by the pro-UFO faction, Klass asked for a referral. Nickell suggested the Yellow Pages.

Checking the Washington directory, Klass came across the name of David Crown, a handwriting expert and former director of the ClA's document authentication division. "I called Crown [now retired] and he told me the MJ–12 papers had been exposed as a hoax," Klass said.

Crown, a self-described "high-priced talent," referred Klass to a New York document analyst with a known interest in the MJ–12 papers—an analyst identified only as "PT." Klass did not know at the time that PT had earlier consulted with Moore, Friedman, and Shandera. He also did not know that PT had already informed Moore that the Truman memo was probably bogus—information Moore was not yet ready to disclose.[11]

Klass telephoned PT, and learned the analyst had a strong interest in seeing a copy of the authentic October 1, 1947, Truman letter. This he mailed via overnight express. There was no mention at the time of PT's involvement with Moore, Friedman, and Shandera.

PT made a transparency of the Truman letter for easy enlargement and carried that, Klass said, along with a transparency of the MJ–12 memo (already in PT's possession), to a document examiner's conference in San Francisco.

"A week later [October 12, 1989], PT called me," Klass recalled. The essence of that conversation was that the MJ–12 document, or at least the

Truman memo, was certainly counterfeit. PT's conclusion—undisputed by other analysts at the West Coast conference—was based, in part, on a comparison of enlarged copies of the two signatures. But there is more.

Klass also learned that PT had been in touch with a Los Angeles document examiner—another man consulting with Moore, Friedman, and Shandera. Months earlier, this analyst had been permitted to reproduce from the original MJ–12 35-mm film.

The availability of first-generation copies, enlarged for comparison and study, enabled PT to firmly conclude that the MJ–12 Truman memo was typed with a Smith Corona *cartridge* machine introduced no earlier than 1963. Clues to determining the typewriter year and model were the capital letters "A" and "W," both of which, Klass said, tended to tear the old style carbon ribbon. This defect was corrected by Smith Corona in the model introduced in 1963.

Which brings us to William Moore's 1989 two-hour talk in Las Vegas.[12] Moore revealed that nine years earlier, in September 1980, he had been approached by a man claiming to be a member of the intelligence community. This individual alleged that he and several others in intelligence were unhappy with the United States Government's UFO cover-up policy. Moore said he was asked to cooperate with this group, and an arrangement was established through a liaison. Moore identified the liaison as Richard Doty, a former special agent with the Air Force Office of Special Investigations (AFOSI). Doty has been retired from the Air Force since 1988.

Moore said it soon became apparent he was being "recruited" by the group to supply information on the activities of a number of UFO researchers, but most especially on a researcher named Paul Bennewitz.

A professional physicist, Bennewitz had been privately investigating UFO and cattle mutilation[13] phenomena, and in the course of this, and using sophisticated electronic equipment, he reportedly intercepted unusual low-frequency radio signals coming from the Kirtland AFB/Sandia National Labs complex in New Mexico. According to Moore, Bennewitz began to speak openly "to virtually anyone" about the signals, convinced that they were UFO and not government connected. Moore claimed that several government agencies became part of an elaborate campaign to "defuse" and discredit Bennewitz by feeding him bizarre misinformation. As a result of this campaign, Bennewitz came to believe that malevolent aliens were hatching a plan to control the Earth. Moore said he decided to play along in order to try to discover more about the government's knowledge of UFOs.

During the course of this, Moore said he was given a document that he was expected to pass along to Bennewitz. This was the "Aquarius" paper referred to earlier—a three-page extract of a longer report supposedly prepared by the mysterious MJ–12 committee. Speaking before MUFON, Moore said the Aquarius paper was a "retyped version" of a "real AFOSI message."[14]

He said the document was handed to him in February 1981 with the intention that he pass it to Bennewitz. It was assumed that Bennewitz would take the document to the media as proof of alien invaders—at which point the paper would be exposed as bogus, and Bennewitz would be further discredited. Moore's disclosure about all of this quite naturally caused an uproar within the UFO community. More to the point is that his admission about the Aquarius paper, when coupled with information supplied by the document analyst PT and by Philip Klass, seems to indicate that very little about the MJ–12 subject is credible. There is, however, another detail which needs be included here—information laid bare, through exhaustive research, by Stanton Friedman.

When MJ–12 first came to light, the UFO community found a surprising name included on the list of alleged "Majestic" members. That name was Dr. Donald H. Menzel.

The reason most found this surprising was because Menzel, a professor of astronomy at Harvard University, waged a lifelong campaign to debunk UFOs. He published three books proclaiming that "flying saucers" were a myth. Menzel died on December 14, 1976, and in the course of his career he never once swerved from an anti-UFO path. Thanks to Friedman's research, there is reason to ask whether Donald Menzel actually had a very different private view of the UFO phenomenon.

Menzel was, in fact, a genius. An astrophysicist, he received his Ph.D. at the age of twenty-three. This alone hardly qualified him to be part of any covert government operation. Indeed, of all those on the MJ–12 list, he was the only one not known to possess a high-level security clearance—but Menzel did have high-level clearance—an Ultra Top Secret Navy clearance.

Friedman tumbled to this information after following a long trail of documents and correspondence that led the late Dr. Menzel past such notables as John

F. Kennedy, Dr. Vannevar Bush, and Dr. Detlev Bronk. (Bush, during World War II, was head of the Office of Scientific Research and Development. Later he headed the Joint Research and Development Board. Bronk was an aviation physiologist and head of the National Academy of Sciences and National Research Council. Both are included on the MJ–12 list.)

The connection between Menzel and Bush was discovered by Friedman soon after he learned about MJ–12. He reported this in his highly-detailed paper, "The Secret Life of Donald H. Menzel," in the January/February 1988 *International UFO Reporter*.[15]

"In checking my files on Vannevar Bush ... I found a letter to Bush from Robert Proctor, a lawyer for the old and established Boston legal firm of Choate, Hall, and Stewart," Friedman wrote. The letter referenced, of all things, loyalty charges brought against Menzel by the United States Air Force. "Suddenly," Friedman continued, "this letter raised a whole host of questions about Menzel."

The loyalty hearings, as Friedman discovered, were convened for a full week in May 1950, with Vannevar Bush firmly in Menzel's camp. Menzel was exonerated of the charges, but the many questions about his past remained. The research trail led Friedman to Mrs. Menzel and to the Harvard Archives in April 1986. "... My findings took me completely by surprise," Friedman wrote. "It is clear that Donald Menzel led two lives."

The nuclear physicist goes on to list nine separate reasons Menzel could have been part of the MJ–12 membership. But the salient facts are these:

- Menzel had a long association with the National Security Agency (NSA)—a fact revealed in letters he wrote to John F. Kennedy in 1960.

- NSA is known to have a UFO connection, and has in fact refused to release 160 UFO documents or even an expurgated version "of a twenty-one-page Top Secret affidavit to a federal judge justifying the withholding of the 160 documents."
- Menzel and Vannevar Bush had a longstanding association "dating back to at least 1934."

Menzel's ties to the National Security Agency are documented in at least three separate letters to Kennedy.[16]

In a letter dated August 13, 1960, he refers to one Oswald Jacoby, noting that he and Jacoby "served in the Navy together, in what is now the National Security Agency. I have been associated with this activity for almost thirty years and probably have the longest continuous record of association in the country."

Menzel further referred to the NSA in an unpublished autobiography,[17] noting that he had been a consultant to the agency, "with Ultra Top Secret clearance ..." Clearly, he did have the background and the above-top-secret clearance necessary for membership into MJ–12—provided the operation ever existed—but many individuals, within and outside of the UFO community, remain unconvinced about any possible connection involving Dr. Menzel.[18] Notable among them is longtime researcher/historian Jerome Clark, who reviewed Friedman's findings in *Fate*.[19]

Clark summarized his view by saying that had Menzel "known something, he would have behaved differently. I doubt that he would have made the public spectacle of himself that he did over two and one-half decades."

He further says: "It is easier to believe he [Menzel] would have used his influence far less visibly to keep colleagues and others away from UFO study. He would have quietly told fellow scientists that his research had convinced him UFOs aren't worth anybody's time ..."

Clark's viewpoint is well considered, but it is one with which I cannot agree. In the scientific community, just as in the UFO research community, there is entirely too much divisiveness. Let one scientist flatly tell another something isn't worth his or her time, and chances are the recipient will set out to prove the other one wrong.

For Menzel, adopting the role of public naysayer was an excellent ruse—a role that cast doubt and disrespect not so much on himself as on the issue. Certainly, his denigrating attitude toward the UFO subject caused a mirrored response among other scientists. This sort of peer pressure is nothing new; it is evident today in business and industry, and even in the UFO community.

In pointing this out, however, I confess to playing devil's advocate. If the MJ–12 papers are a sham, as they seem to be, then Dr. Menzel could not have been part of this "operation." My suspicion is that the document was manufactured by someone fully aware of Menzel's high-level clearance, and who intentionally included his name. Without doing a ton of research, as Stan Friedman did, only someone with ready access to secure files would have been able to ferret out that particular detail—which brings us to Roswell, New Mexico.

Consider: The MJ–12 document surfaced at a time when Roswell was a hot topic. Moore and Friedman had already compiled extensive evidence of a forty-year-old occurrence near the community. It is apparent the Army Air Corps was involved: that news reports were issued, then altered. There is every indication of a major cover-up, but of what? An alien spacecraft? Or was it something else?

Consider: Kenneth Arnold never reported seeing "flying saucers" over the Cascade Mountains two weeks prior to the alleged Roswell crash. His description, at least for the lead object in the formation, was more like that of a flying wing or flying crescent. A news reporter coined the expression "flying saucer."

Consider also: In 1947, Northrop Corporation had been testing prototype flying wings for at least a year (as related in the opening chapter). Northrop has never released any of the early flying wings for permanent public display. (The two prototypes crashed, but a number of other flying wings were built.) It is likely the test models were kept secure because Northrop continued to work with, and improve upon, the basic design—leading, ultimately, to the development of the modern B–2 stealth bomber.

Despite all this, I am not saying (nor do I really believe) that an early flying wing crashed in New Mexico in 1947.[20] I use the wing as an example of how little we really know about military research and development during this era. What I am suggesting is that the government had something more advanced in the works—something that may have failed miserably on a hot day in early July, 1947.

In March 1995, the Department of Defense declassified "Silver Bug," a project that had been under wraps since its inception shortly after World War II. A report on the project, dated February 15, 1955, reveals plans and designs for a saucer-shaped vertical lift vehicle which, in theory, would fly at speeds of 2,300 miles per hour at an altitude of eighty thousand feet. The plans were said to have been inspired by designs taken from the Germans at the end of World War II. The Germans were unable to complete work on "Silver Bug," but it's possible that a fully operational prototype was built and tested in the United States. It is also conceivable that a test flight of the prototype ended in a crash near Roswell.

In the wake of the crash, and with public opinion about flying discs shifting toward a belief in alien spacecraft, a two-part disinformation scheme was set into motion.

Designed to capitalize on the saucer craze, the scheme began with an announcement to radio and press that a flying disc had been recovered. To the media, this implied a spacecraft or, at least, a new type of Russian aircraft, inasmuch as tension between the United States and the Soviets had begun to develop. The second phase was the "cover-up." This involved quashing the "genuine" disc report and replacing it with a clumsy account about a fallen weather balloon. The result was that a segment of the public—accustomed to wartime secrecy—decided the first story was true: a disc—a spaceship, perhaps—had been recovered. Those who didn't believe in alien visitors simply accepted the balloon story. Few, then or now, ever considered that the crash might have involved the test of a top-secret American aircraft.

This still leaves us with the witnesses and their descendants—men and women who claim hieroglyphic-like writing was seen on pieces of wreckage, who insist that the wreckage fragments were of an unknown metal alloy, and who even claim that alien bodies were recovered at the scene (bringing to mind a certain well-known "alien autopsy" film, but we'll come back to this). Possibly, the witness recollection is a "screen"—a false memory instilled by the deceivers through the use of drugs and hypnosis. Or perhaps it is simply what some wish to remember. There are, of course, many who would argue this. Researchers such as Donald R. Schmitt and Kevin D. Randle,[21] as well as Stan Friedman,[22] have all spent considerable time investigating the Roswell incident. While they disagree on details, they are all nonetheless fairly certain that an alien vehicle crashed and that bodies were recovered. The point here is that tales of the event are not enough. Hard evidence is necessary.

In early 1993, Steven Schiff, a Republican congressman from New Mexico and a colonel in the Air Force Reserve, was asked by several constituents to look into the Roswell story. Schiff took them seriously enough to begin an inquiry. In March 1993 he wrote to then-Secretary of Defense Les Aspin, asking for a personal briefing and a report on all actions regarding Roswell. Schiff received replies from Colonel Larry G. Shockley, of the office of the Assistant Secretary of Defense for legislative affairs, and from Rudy de Leon, Special Assistant to the Defense Secretary. Both men referred Schiff to the National Archives and Record Administration.

Schiff again wrote to Aspin in May and August, and demanded that the Defense Department conduct the necessary research to produce a detailed report. At one point he received a letter from R. Michael McReynolds, director of the textual reference division of the National Archives. McReynolds said the Air Force had turned over to the archives all records of its investigation into UFOs, but nothing in that investigation, called Project Blue Book, said anything about Roswell. Schiff's media response was that his search was "... not a UFO hunt. This is a file hunt. The idea of alien spacecraft is not my first explanation for any of this. It's possible it was a weather balloon, attended by a public relations fiasco."

In early 1994, Schiff—still unable to get answers—asked Congress' investigative arm, the General Accounting Office, to look into the matter. Meanwhile, the Air Force issued a whole new report of its own on Roswell—reiterating that the crashed object was nothing more than a research balloon. In mid-summer of 1995, the GAO report was released, but it resolved nothing—the balloon explanation went unaltered. One curious fact of the probe, however, was the discovery that many of the old Roswell Army Air Field records were somehow destroyed. In fact, more than three years worth of records are said to be lost, including any and all RAAF documents from the June to July 1947 period.

In late 1995, the appearance of a bizarre video eclipsed the long-awaited GAO report. Created from 16-mm film obtained by a London, England, music promoter named Ray Santilli, the video purports to show the autopsy of an extraterrestrial body taken from the Roswell crash site. Santilli reported that he purchased the film from an unidentified man who claimed he was a military cameraman at Roswell.

The film is said to be old stock—possibly 1947 stock. Nonetheless, it is regarded with suspicion: ufologists, medical experts, and professional filmmakers have all demonstrated serious differences of opinion on whether the film is authentic or an elaborate, expensive hoax. If authentic, why is it not in government hands? The mysterious cameraman supposedly held back certain canisters of film because of difficulty in processing. Other canisters—the majority, apparently—were processed and sent directly to Washington.

Later, when the problem film was ready, the cameraman reportedly tried—without success—to have his Washington contacts come and get it. Why would they completely disregard the additional film? And how did it pass, eventually and easily, into the hands of someone who would make it public? Even if long overlooked by those privy to such secrets, then at the first whisper of its disclosure the film most likely would have disappeared for good. If there is a cover-up in place since 1947, then the autopsy film was a tremendous blunder—a major break in an otherwise tightly woven web of security.

How, exactly, does all this fit with the MJ–12 document? Actually, it's pretty simple.

Whoever masterminded the document (and perhaps even the autopsy film) was simply taking advantage of the legend surrounding Roswell, and didn't in fact much care whether a UFO crashed near there in 1947 or not. Why do I say this? Because no matter what happened at Roswell, it panders to those who wish to believe—it reinforces the already widespread notion that our planet is being visited by extraterrestrials.

Who stands to gain from this? How about members of the counterintelligence community?

Fostering this sort of belief makes an excellent cover for covert types; they can perform all sorts of unscrupulous activity—abductions and experimentation, for example—and with hypnosis and drugs and who knows what other techniques, pass it off as the actions of meddling, superior, unstoppable alien beings.

Because a document such as MJ–12 is so nearly believable, even after close scrutiny and when it is found to be wanting, it generates suspicion and frustration among all concerned. In the end no one knows with any certainty what to believe and everyone ends up growling at one another. Indeed, emotional storms such as this have long kept the UFO community in the United States so fragmented that its members can never hope to accomplish much of anything.

As for the Roswell legend, the only thing certain is that something happened in the desert in 1947: something important, something requiring military intervention and a heavy mantle of secrecy. The truth, as they say, may be out there, but in this instance it may be well out of reach.

NOTES

5. Curt Sutherly, "MJ–12: Evidence of Deception," *Caveat Emptor*, spring 1990, edited by Gene Steinberg, pp. 13–20.

6. *San Francisco Chronicle*, July 9, 1947.

7. Leonard Lee Rue III, *Complete Guide to Game Animals, second revised edition* (New York: Outdoor Life Books, 1981), p. 15.

8. Curt Sutherly, "An Interview with Stanton Friedman," *Official UFO*, May 1977.

9. Many of the "White Papers" disseminated by Phil Klass are photocopied letters addressed to those he has challenged. Moore, Friedman, and Doty have all been recipients of such letters.

10. A letter to William Moore.

11. Information about the apparently bogus Truman memo was not released by MF&S, according to Moore, because the trio had pursued

"several opinions" to lend credibility to their findings. However, these opinions were "mixed." (Letter from Moore to Klass dated October 16, 1989.)

12. William L. Moore's presentation was given July 1, 1989, at the Aladdin Hotel, Las Vegas.

13. Cattle and other livestock have been found dead with organs, eyes, ears, or tongues removed and blood often drained from the body. The mutilations have frustrated law enforcement officials who have been unable to halt the killing or even identify the perpetrators. The mutilations began attracting widespread media attention in 1967, when an Appaloosa pony named "Snippy" was found dead in the San Luis Valley, Colorado.

14. Moore allegedly admitted to researcher Richard Hall that he personally did a "cut and paste job" on the Aquarius paper. (Robert Hastings, "The MJ–12 Affair: Facts, Questions, Comments," *MUFON UFO Journal*, June 1989, p. 8.

15. *International UFO Reporter,* publication of the Center For UFO Studies, Chicago, Illinois. Additional information can be found in Stanton Friedman's 108-page "Final Report On Operation Majestic 12" (May 1990, UFORI, P.O. Box 958, Houlton, ME 04730-0958).

16. The Kennedy letters were located by Stanton Friedman among various Menzel papers at the Harvard University Archives. Friedman received permission to review the papers from the chairman of the Harvard astronomy department and the director of the Smithsonian Observatory.

17. In April 1986, Friedman reviewed Dr. Menzel's autobiography after receiving permission from the widow, Florence Menzel.

18. Mrs. Menzel has dismissed Friedman's theory about a possible MJ–12 association. (Letter from Mrs. Menzel to James Moseley, *Saucer Smear*, February 5, 1989.)

19. Jerome Clark, "Who Was Donald Menzel?" *Fate*, August 1989. Clark was the longtime writer of "UFO Reporter," a regular column in *Fate*. His final entry appeared in the May 1993 issue.

20. Prototype and experimental aircraft were tested at Muroc Field (Edwards AFB) in 1947, and at China Lake, California. There was no known testing of aircraft in New Mexico.

21. Kevin D. Randle and Donald R. Schmitt, co-authors of *The UFO Crash at Roswell* (New York: Avon Books, 1991), and *The Truth About the UFO Crash at Roswell* (New York: M. Evans and Company, 1994).

22. Stanton T. Friedman and Don Berliner, *Crash At Corona* (New York: Paragon House, 1992).

Chapter Five:

Dark Moons, Red World

Somewhere in space, presumably near Mars and possibly even in Mars orbit, is a dysfunctional robot spacecraft. A one billion dollar spacecraft: the Mars Observer.

Launched from Florida on September 25, 1992, the Observer spent nearly a year coasting through space, arriving in the neighborhood of Mars on August 21, 1993. Equipped with numerous backup systems and fail safes, it was the most sophisticated machine ever sent to the red planet, and the first United States probe directed to Mars in seventeen years. It was scheduled to enter orbit on August 24, 1993, and then spend the next seventy-five days maneuvering into a near-polar orbit 234 miles high.

From polar orbit, the Observer was programmed to activate its instruments and conduct a photo-reconnaissance of the entire planet. It was also programmed to take extensive readings of the surface and measurements of the thin Martian atmosphere.

As the Observer approached the red planet, its radio was turned off so that a filament in a delicate transmitter tube would be protected during pressurization of the thruster fuel tanks. When the time came for the transmitter to be turned back on, there was only silence. With the deadline slipping by for entering orbit, mission engineers signaled the Observer to activate its backup transmitter.[23] There was no response. Then, hoping the craft had entered orbit but was unable to receive commands (due, perhaps, to a faulty radio receiver), they waited—knowing that after five days and no message from Earth, the Observer was programmed to radio mission control and ask, in effect, "Why aren't you talking to me?"[24] Again, there was only silence as another unmanned probe was lost near Mars.

In March 1989, the Soviet Mars probe, Fobos 2, went mysteriously silent. But unlike the Mars Observer, Fobos 2 sent back a string of data and a number of photographs before mission control in Kaliningrad lost contact. Some of these photos revealed "enigmatic" objects and surface features that continue to puzzle space scientists.

At the time, journalists in the United States joked that perhaps the Red Star was not compatible with the red planet.[25] The Russians had already lost Fobos 1, the companion craft to Fobos 2, and questions were raised about the level of competence of this latest Mars venture.

Indeed, the history of unmanned exploration of Mars has been, for the Russians, one of frequent misfortune. As early as 1963, the Soviet probe, Mars 1, went dead at a distance of about 133 million miles from the sun. In 1965, the Soviet probe, Zond 2, went dead, this time at a distance of about 128 million miles from the sun. Neither craft was ever heard from again.[26] Other Russian probes to follow either encountered difficulty or vanished.

While the loss of these probes posed a huge setback for the Russians, the problem was not uniquely theirs. Spacecraft launched by the United States were also going awry en route to Mars.

In 1964, the United States Mariner 3 failed shortly after liftoff. The following year the Mariner 4 experienced control problems in roughly the same area of space as the Mars 1 and Zond 2. Fortunately, in this case, control was reestablished and Mariner 4 went on to be a success—but trouble struck again four years later in July 1969. This time it was with the Mariner 7, intended to fly within two thousand miles of the red planet. Engineers at the Jet Propulsion Laboratory (JPL) in Pasadena, California, suddenly lost contact with the craft. Then, some seven hours later the probe came alive, though its ability to transmit data was somewhat decreased and its velocity slightly increased![27]

At the time this occurred, two reporters for *Time* magazine, Don Neff and David Lee, were covering the Mariner 7 mission. In their rather fertile imagination, this latest occurrence suggested the presence of a "great galactic ghoul" sitting in space near Mars. The ghoul, they decided, had eaten the earlier Soviet probes and swallowed Mariner 7, but for some reason didn't like the taste and spit it back out.[28] Today the Great Galactic Ghoul is a joke that has become something of a space-age legend.

Like ancient mariners confronted with vanishing ships and vast uncharted oceans who posted on their maps "Beyond This Place There Be Dragons," or like the test pilots of the 1940s who spoke of a sonic "wall in the sky" that prevented aircraft from going faster than sound, the explorers of space (and those who chronicle them) are giving rise to new myths and legends. No one takes the ghoul seriously, but neither can anyone dismiss the fact that something odd is happening out near Mars.

On the night of August 11, 1877, astronomer Asaph Hall perched himself at the eyepiece of the newly completed twenty-six-inch telescope at the United States Naval Observatory, Washington, D.C., and pointed it in the direction of Mars. Hall was searching for two Martian moons which had long been described in legend and folklore. That night, unlike previous nights, his efforts paid off as he spotted a faint object not far from Mars itself.

Unfortunately for Hall, the weather became overcast later that evening and it wasn't until the night of August 16, 1877, that he was again able to locate the object, which proved to be a Martian satellite.

On the following night, August 17, Hall made an additional discovery—another satellite even closer to the red planet. He named the outer moon Deimos, and the inner one Phobos.

In 1944, another United States Naval Observatory astronomer, B. P. Sharpless, began gathering together all the available observational data on the moons of Mars.[29] His intention was to determine, as best as possible, the orbits of the two satellites. What he discovered was a surprise.

Sharpless found that the inner moon, Phobos, appeared to be in a very gradually decaying orbit. In astronomical parlance, this is called "secular acceleration." Artificial satellites undergo secular acceleration—falling slowly at first, but gradually picking up speed—until they meet a fiery end in the Earth's atmosphere. Sharpless, who later reexamined his calculations, remained convinced that Phobos was in a slow, decaying orbit. Despite this, the matter was given little serious consideration and eventually relegated to the astronomical gossip columns.

In July 1988, the former Soviet Union launched Fobos 1 and Fobos 2 from the Baikonur Cosmodrome.[30] The two probes were the most advanced ever sent by that nation, costing roughly $480 million. At first all went well during the two hundred-day mission, but during a scheduled talk with Fobos 1 on September 2, 1988, the craft failed to respond. Later, the Russians said the problem was caused by a mistaken command relayed by a radio operator. A month passed while they tried to restore communications, to no avail.

The backup craft, Fobos 2, meanwhile continued on toward Mars without difficulty. En route, the robot vehicle studied (as had its companion) the composition of the "solar wind"—the charged particles blowing from the Sun, which theorists believe could be used to power manned craft harnessed to huge mirrored sails. Also studied were the characteristics of interplanetary shock waves and the location of gamma ray outbursts. Arriving at Mars, Fobos 2 entered a temporary orbit. Had all gone as planned, it would have later shifted to an "observational" orbit in order to begin a study of the moon Phobos—the main mission target.

Along with Deimos, its sister moon, Phobos has been of interest to the Russians since about 1960. That year the astrophysicist, I. S. Shklovskii, began to reexamine the discoveries made by the astronomer

Sharpless. The Russian was puzzled by the earlier man's findings. He did not dispute them, but in trying to understand the decaying orbit, he eliminated one possible cause after another. He ruled out the influence of the gravitational fields of Mars and the sun on the orbit of the moon. And he calculated that, at ten miles across, Phobos should be too massive to be dragged down by the thin Martian atmosphere. What's more, Mars has no known magnetic field to influence the moon. The only explanation, Shklovskii finally reasoned, was that Phobos has a very low density; it is not as massive as it appears, and is thus susceptible to atmospheric drag.

Slowed by this drag, Phobos would begin to creep toward Mars—the onset of secular acceleration, but when the scientist calculated the necessary value, he found the impossible. In order to be affected by the thin Martian atmosphere, Phobos would need a density akin to one one-thousandth the density of water.[31] Since there is no natural substance with such a low density, he concluded that Phobos had to be hollow—and therefore, perhaps artificial!

In his book, *The Cosmic Connection*, Cornell University astronomer Carl Sagan made the following observations:

> With such a low density, there was only one conclusion possible. Phobos had to be hollow. A vast hollow object 10 miles across could not have arisen by natural processes. Shklovskii, therefore, concluded that it was produced by an advanced Martian civilization. Indeed, an artificial satellite 10 miles across requires a technology far in advance of our own.[32]

In 1971, the unmanned Mariner 9 spacecraft achieved Mars orbit—arriving, unfortunately, at a time when the red planet's surface was masked by a massive dust storm. For Sagan, the storm proved a blessing, as he was able to convince NASA to swing the camera scan platforms of the spacecraft toward the Martian moons. Prior to this, Sagan had spent a year lobbying space administration officials to grant him a look at the two moons. NASA had been reluctant to change the Mariner mission profile, and Sagan's request would most likely never have been granted had it not been for the unexpected dust storm.[33]

On the night of November 30, 1971, Sagan and a former student, Dr. Joseph Veverka, for the first time were able to observe close-up photographs of Phobos. After the image was enhanced by computer, Sagan pronounced the moon as looking "not so much like an artificial satellite as a diseased potato." He described the orbiting moon as battered, extensively cratered, and "probably billions of years old." He added, "There is no sign of technology on it."[34]

Additional photographs of the moon later did reveal something unusual: a system of linear surface grooves, each about one-third mile across and roughly parallel. These grooves, geologists decided in 1978, are probably "surface manifestations of deep-seated fractures,"[35] though the cause of the deep fractures is still uncertain.

Five years after Mariner 9 sent back the first revealing photographs, the mass of Phobos was measured for the first time during a series of fly-bys made by the Viking I spacecraft.[36] Based on this measurement, the density was determined to be quite low, though not nearly as low as was calculated by Shklovskii. Not enough, at any rate, to support a theory that Phobos is hollow (which leaves the cause of the decaying orbit again unexplained). Viking I also verified a suspicion that both Phobos and its sister moon, Deimos, are extremely dark in color.

The information on color and density, along with other data transmitted by the probe in May 1977, led scientists to conclude that the moons are made of water-rich carbonaceous chondrite. Found only in the most primitive of meteorites, carbonaceous chondrite is possibly the nearest thing to the original dust from which the moons and planets were formed. Meteors made of the stuff are thought to originate in the asteroid belt between Mars and Jupiter. If Phobos and Deimos are made of carbonaceous chondrite, then they probably originated in the belt and were later captured by Mars.

More than two thousand asteroids, or minor planets, have been identified out in the dark space between Mars and Jupiter. They range in size from a few miles to more than six hundred miles in diameter, and there are certainly many still undiscovered. The asteroids may once have been part of a larger whole, a major planet. The Martian moons, Phobos and Deimos, may be two pieces of the debris from that world.

The belief that a planet once existed between Mars and Jupiter is an old one, though there is another more recent view—a theory that asteroids are pieces of a world that never fully formed. While no one really knows which view (if either) is correct, the destroyed world theory seems to be the more popular of the two notions. Its proponents suggest that a planet orbiting between Mars and Jupiter exploded, or was struck by another large body (possibly a comet), sending fragments hurtling into surrounding space. How long ago this may have happened is anyone's guess—millions, or billions, of years may have passed in the interim. Of the many fragments, some—a few, perhaps—had sufficient kinetic energy to begin a slow drift toward the sun. Along the way they encountered Mars, and two of the asteroids were snared by that gravitational field and drawn into orbit, becoming the moons Phobos and Deimos. There is, however, another possibility.

According to a NASA report titled *Mars As Viewed by Mariner 9*, meteorites and asteroids are frequently light in color. The Martian moons are extremely dark and evidently of a different composition—the carbonaceous chondrite material which, in meteorites of that composition, contains up to twenty percent water.[37] Now, assume for a moment that, ages ago, Mars was inhabited. A higher intelligence on the planet would have noticed the passing asteroids and almost certainly coveted their value. To the resident population, the asteroids would have been a tremendous boon—a source of water and raw material.

A sufficiently advanced people would have been able to shepherd the asteroids into a stable orbit, and then begin extensive mining and percolation operations to extract water and raw ore. The fact that our space probes have spotted no evidence of this does not eliminate the possibility. If the significant tunneling, engineering, and mining were done deep in the stone, need there be much evidence on the surface?

The idea that someone may have been mining or excavating small worlds in our solar system is not new. For years, rumors have persisted about the discovery of this sort of activity on Earth's own satellite.

In the 1970s, a writer named George H. Leonard compiled a book boldly titled *Somebody Else Is on the Moon* (David McKay Company, Inc., 1976). Leonard claimed that a thorough study of NASA photographs revealed the presence of alien machinery on the lunar surface. Also revealed, he said, were changes deliberately made in the landscape, and some suspicion of mining or excavating activities. He cited an anonymous informant: an engineer with a Ph.D. in physics formerly employed by NASA. The mystery informant supported Leonard's claim (perhaps a little too conveniently) by explaining that he and others working for NASA were well aware of something odd occurring on the moon. Leonard concluded that it was the suspicion or discovery of this alien presence that triggered the space race between the United States and the USSR.

Some years prior to the release of Leonard's book, in 1971, I was told of an unusual occurrence during one of the manned Apollo lunar missions. At the time I was a young sergeant in the United States Air Force, and the man who told the story is a former astronaut who shall go unnamed. On this particular mission, he said the main craft entered lunar orbit and the lander vehicle separated and began its descent. During the descent, the lander maintained normal radio communication with the orbiting command vehicle. Then something unexpected happened.

The astronaut noted that bizarre sounds, like fire engine sirens, singing, and a generally unintelligible chatter broke in on the restricted NASA radio band. Later, when the lander was en route back to the command module, the strange interference ceased. However, when the Apollo crew radioed

Houston and asked if Mission Control had monitored the unusual racket, the response was, in effect:
"No, if you're picking up strange sounds, they're
local in nature."

Years later, I learned that some of these odd noises
were believed by NASA technicians to be interference
between the command module's and lander's VHF
radios. But that explanation doesn't take into account
the variety of sounds described by the astronaut.

During the mid-1970s, I experienced something
quite like this noise phenomenon. While discussing a
story idea with an editor by telephone, the long distance call was suddenly interrupted by a barrage of
sound—a combination of loud chattering mixed with
bell tones, sirens, and much more. The noise was
frightening and caused the editor to terminate the
conversation quickly.

Since 1898, when H. G. Wells's *War of the Worlds*
caught the imagination of the English literary set, stories about Mars have been a staple of science fiction.
The *John Carter* novels of Edgar Rice Burroughs,
Robert Heinlein's *Red Planet*, Ray Bradbury's *The
Martian Chronicles*, and Ben Bova's *Mars* are but a
few of the novels and short stories written about our
mysterious neighbor in space.

A far older work of fiction—Jonathan Swift's legendary satire, *Gulliver's Travels*—contains a startling
reference to the moons of Mars. While the reference
is quite brief, no more than a half paragraph, it is
astounding in that Swift's book was originally published in 1726—*more than 150 years before the discovery of the two moons by astronomer Asaph Hall.*

In Part III of his lengthy satire,[38] Swift places his
hero, Gulliver, on the floating island of Laputa,

where astronomers are hard at work mapping the heavens. Of the astronomers and their work, Gulliver proclaims:

> "They have made a catalogue of ten thousand fixed stars ... They have likewise discovered two lesser stars, or 'satellites,' which revolve about Mars, whereof the innermost is distant from the center of the primary planet exactly three of his diameters, and the outermost five; the former revolves in the space of ten hours, and the latter in twenty-one and an half ..."

Most modern scholars believe Swift "borrowed" his information about the Martian satellites from calculations made by Johannes Kepler, the sixteenth-century discoverer of the laws of planetary motion, who is also frequently credited with having discovered the moons of Mars. However, Kepler merely speculated that Mars had two moons; he based this on a belief that since Venus had no moons and Earth had one, then Mars, accordingly, should have two. Out of this grew a belief that each consecutive planet in the solar system possessed one additional moon. This belief was reinforced when the four largest moons of Jupiter were discovered. Mercury was still unknown, and the (hypothetically) ruined fifth planet, where the asteroid belt is located, would have had three moons by this method of reasoning. Today we know this planetary "law" is nonsense, but Kepler couldn't have known that.

This, however, creates a paradox: if Kepler didn't have specific information pertaining to the two Martian moons, then how did Swift come by the calculations given in *Gulliver's Travels*? To restate, he has the inner moon traveling about the planet in ten hours, and the outer moon in twenty-one and one half hours. The actual orbital time for each moon is:

Phobos, seven hours, thirty-nine minutes; Deimos, thirty hours, eighteen minutes.

In an article published in *Pursuit*,[39] the journal of the Society for the Investigation of the Unexplained, former editor Robert J. Durant writes: "Swift's accuracy leaves something to be desired, but his figures are nevertheless 'in the ballpark.' One familiar with the history [of that era of astronomy] would be slow to fault Swift."

Possibly there is an ancient record somewhere documenting the orbit and position of each Martian moon. Outside of recent times, our knowledge of history is terribly incomplete: what we know of our own distant past is largely guesswork propped up by a carefully cultivated belief structure. We may have climbed and fallen time and again, with each civilization rediscovering the knowledge of the past. The solar system may have been mapped and explored, and even colonized, in an earlier age. Evidence of this, if any, would probably be found on Mars or on either of its two tiny moons.

Discoveries pointing to the existence of ancient, highly advanced civilizations have never met with much enthusiasm from the scientific community. Most are quietly brushed aside and conveniently forgotten. One example is the controversial Piri Re'is map discovered during the early part of this century.[40] This map and innumerable artifacts found through the years provide strong evidence of earlier advanced societies—but did these civilizations originate on Earth, or somewhere else? The "ancient astronaut" champions would have us believe that humanity originated elsewhere in the galaxy and settled here, or at least visited Earth for a time—planting the seeds of civilization. Then again, if mankind came from space, perhaps it was from somewhere much nearer. Perhaps *Homo sapiens* originated on Mars.

Consider: About twelve thousand years ago, Mars was a far warmer planet than it is today, with a heavier atmosphere capable of sustaining life of the order now found on Earth. This is not a vague speculation, but rather an idea entertained by some of today's leading space scientists. At some point an ice age began, accompanied by greatly lowered surface pressure. Liquid water started to vaporize, and eventually, much of the Martian atmosphere became locked away in polar ice caps.

What might have caused this climate change is not known, though the slow, processional movement of the planets through the solar system may have finally carried Mars too far from the sun. Caught in this change, a civilized race would have been forced to take drastic measures to avoid collapse or annihilation. A few may have escaped, fleeing inward to a warmer, wilder planet third from the sun. In doing so, they would have left their world dying, their cities crumbling—and on the surface of two dark moons, perhaps, some trace of their final passing.

The probe Fobos 2, in 1989, was clearly intended to search for evidence of anything odd or unnatural on the inner moon. Arguments stating otherwise are weakened by knowledge of the unusual planning that went into the project, and by the Russian predilection that Phobos is hollow.

Programmed to spend some two months maneuvering close to the Martian moon, the probe would have eventually conducted experiments from a distance of only 160 feet above the surface. It would also have dropped two modules to the surface.

The modules were designed to study soil content, measure the magnetic field of Phobos, and relay panoramic views of the moon's surface. Afterward, Fobos 2 was to return to Mars and begin a prolonged orbital study.

But, of course, none of this came to pass. After entering a temporary Mars orbit, Fobos 2 transmitted images of the planet's surface. It also sent back a good deal of data on the Martian environment. Then, on March 27, 1989, on schedule, it broke radio link with Kaliningrad in order to take photographs of Phobos that would later assist mission planners in plotting a trajectory there. At the close of the photo session, the craft was programmed to turn its high-gain antenna back toward Earth. Instead, Kaliningrad received only a brief, weak signal, after which Fobos 2 went silent, apparently forever.[41]

The photos sent back only deepened the mystery. One showed a system of straight lines about the planet's equator that look like cracks in dry earth.[42] However, since the camera was loaded with infrared film, scientists concluded that the lines were not a geological feature but were instead a vast source of heat. Each line was estimated to be about three to four kilometers wide. Another photo showed an oblong shadow, quite regular in its features, and quite large. However, the object casting the shadow—something obviously huge—was not visible in the photo.

The final photo, televised on the original *Sightings* series on FOX–TV, was a view not of the planet, but of space. Taken just before all contact was lost with Fobos 2, it showed an object in space that no one can identify.

* * *

Photographs of the red planet taken by the two Viking orbiters in 1976 disclosed many startling Martian features, including some strongly suggestive of pyramids. From above, they look amazingly like our own terrestrial pyramids—an apex with four or more sloping sides. The "official" explanation for these formations is they are mountain peaks sculpted by powerful, aberrant air currents.

Another strange feature is a vast belt of sand dunes encircling the Martian north pole which, according to researchers, may be the largest dune belt in the solar system.

More intriguing still is an enigma at the edge of the polar ice cap dubbed "the searchlight" by NASA scientists. This is an area formed by "two diverging straight lines" between which the Martian surface is completely different from that of the surrounding terrain. No one has offered a conclusive statement regarding the "searchlight," and it is doubtful that anyone will anytime soon. However, the man who was Viking orbiter imaging team leader, Michael H. Carr of the United States Geological Survey, made a statement at the time of discovery that "there appears to be some translucent cover over this region ..."

Thirty-two months after the disappearance of Fobos 2, a strange object approached and passed within 288,000 miles of Earth. The object was first spotted with a small telescope on November 6, 1991, at Kitt Peak, Arizona. Believed to be an asteroid, continued observations revealed that it had a curious tendency to "wink"—that is, to become three times brighter, then dark again, every seven and one half minutes. This led to speculation that the object was an artificial satellite, or even a spacecraft of some kind.

As the object continued to approach, it was tracked by astronomers using a sixty-inch telescope at the European Southern Observatory in La Silla, Chile. Accurate measurements of the "winking" confirmed that the phenomenon was reminiscent of the pulsations of light observed on reflective, rapidly rotating satellites. The astronomers tracking the object were Richard West, Olivier Hainaut, and Alain Smette.

The mystery object came closest to Earth on December 5, after which it began drifting away. It was estimated to be about thirty feet in diameter. By the end of the month there were no further reports about the object.

Three days after the Mars Observer was scheduled to enter orbit, mission planners at JPL glumly concluded that the one billion dollar probe was gone, probably irretrievably lost.[43] Speculation abounded: the Observer was in orbit as planned, but was unable to contact Earth due to a faulty transistor in the craft's central clock. The probe failed to make orbit and went sailing off into interplanetary space. The oxygen/hydrazine propellant tanks ruptured during pressurization, destroying the craft.

The explosion theory, raised by observers outside the actual project, was frowned upon by JPL engineers. During a news conference at JPL, Glenn E. Cunningham, project director, said an explosion from overpressurization was highly unlikely due to various backup systems.[44] Sources outside said that although the probe was equipped with backup pressure regulators, the regulators would not have prevented a problem caused by an abrupt surge in pressure.

Meanwhile, fringe groups began announcing that the probe was still intact, and transmitting on schedule. They claimed the transmitted data was being kept from the public because it revealed an alien presence on or around Mars.

In truth, any suggestion of intelligent life, past or present, on the red planet would have been easily spotted and recorded by the Mars Observer. An on-board camera designed by geologist Michael Malin, of Arizona State University, would have allowed close-up photos of individual Martian features.[45] Costing thirteen million dollars, the camera was powerful enough to obtain clear images of automobile-sized objects on the surface—objects such as the Viking landers sitting there since 1976, which NASA intended to photograph.

Other planned photos would have included close-ups of the famous "face" on Mars, located not far from the pyramids in the northern desert region known as Cydonia. Long regarded by geologists as nothing more than a curiosity of the Martian landscape, the "face" bears a remarkable resemblance to a human visage peering skyward. The Mars Observer would have revealed, once and for all, the truth about this and other enigmatic features.

In early September 1993, only a week after the loss of the Mars Observer, the United States and Russia announced an "unprecedented" space exploration agreement.[46] The terms of the agreement, signed by Vice President Al Gore and Prime Minister Victor Chernomyrdin, permit the pooling of technical and financial resources of each country in matters of manned space exploration. The agreement is expected to hasten the development of the over-budget space station Freedom, and perhaps pave the way for joint manned missions to the moon and Mars.

Hopefully, within the decade ahead the long overdue manned mission to Mars will become a reality—though current funding difficulties make this doubtful.

As for the Great Galactic Ghoul or whatever it is that seems to be interfering with our robot probes: to date, the best explanation put forward by NASA—an explanation that sounds a bit lame nonetheless—is that the various craft are encountering a cloud of tiny particles, or space dust, out near Mars—particles that could affect the delicate trajectory and instrumentation of the probes.

Or perhaps the problem is merely an incredible run of bad luck, both for the United States and the Russians. If not, and there is also no natural phenomenon at work, then it would almost seem that someone—or something—is intentionally interfering with our efforts to take a close, careful look at Mars.

We humans are stubborn, and sooner or later we'll have our close look. When we do, will we find evidence of some non-human culture? Or discover, instead, the ruins of our own ancient past?

NOTES

23. John Noble Wilford, "Gloom is Growing Over The Outcome of a Mars Mission," *New York Times*, August 24, 1993, p. C5.
24. Wilford, "A Craft Nearing Mars Sends Back Only Silence, and Hope Dwindles," *New York Times*, August 25, 1993, p. A11.
25. Les Dorr, Jr., "Fobos Phlops," *Final Frontier*, August 1989, p. 7.
26. "The Great Galactic Ghoul," *Pursuit*, October 1972 [reprinted from *The National Observer*,

November 13, 1971, "Mars and a Space Age Gremlin"], p. 80.

27. Ibid., p. 80.
28. Ibid, p. 80; also James E. Oberg, "The Great Galactic Ghoul," *Final Frontier*, October 1989, p. 10.
29. Carl Sagan, *The Cosmic Connection* (New York: Dell Publishing, 1973), p. 106.
30. Vyacheslav Kovtunenko, technical director, Russian Fobos project, "Next Stop Phobos," *Final Frontier*, April 1989, pp. 32, 36.
31. Carl Sagan, *The Cosmic Connection*, p. 106.
32. Ibid, pp. 106–107.
33. Ibid, p. 107.
34. Ibid, pp. 108–109.
35. "Origin Of The Grooves On Phobos," *Nature*, No.273, pp. 282–284.
36. "Tidal Stresses Made Phobos Groovy," *New Scientist*, No.74, p. 394.
37. Ibid, p. 394.
38. Jonathan Swift, *Gulliver's Travels and Other Writings* (New York: Bantam Books, 1986) p. 168.
39. Robert J. Durant, "The Moons of Mars," *Pursuit*, January 1973, p. 11.
40. The map of Piri Ibn Haji Memmed. Piri was a Turkish admiral, a "re'is" in his own language, though the word is usually misspelled as "reis." His map was discovered in 1929 and a copy sent to President Wilson in 1930. A second copy was sent to the United States Navy Hydrographic Office in 1956. The map shows, in clear delineation, both the east and west coasts of South America; and yet it was drawn by Piri (or ordered drawn by him) only twenty years after Cristobal Colon (Christopher Columbus) made his first trip across the Atlantic. Piri Re'is

claimed he copied the western coastline of South America from a map taken from a captured member of Colon's crew in 1513—*the same year the explorer Balboa sailed into the Pacific*. The source material for these maps— those in the possession of Colon and his men, and Piri's own—is thought to have been still earlier maps drawn during the twelfth and fourteenth centuries, found in Hebrew seminaries. If this is true, Colon was almost certainly aware that new lands lay to the West. What makes these ancient maps so much the more astonishing is that they reveal certain aerial features of islands in the Arctic region—Ellesmere Island and other Northern Canadian islands—which were completely unknown until the United States Air Force conducted a classified aerial survey in the 1950s. Moreover, they reveal a clearly delineated view of Queen Maud Land in the Antarctic region—*a region apparently mapped before it became ice-covered*. The topographical details of this area were only rediscovered somewhat recently, through seismological soundings of one and one-half-mile thick ice. A definitive history of the Piri Re'is map is contained in Professor Charles H. Hapgood's 1966 *Maps of the Ancient Sea Kings*.

Interested readers are also directed to the late Louis L'Amour's novel, *The Walking Drum*, which, though a fictional work, contains many carefully researched, non-fictional references to early Eastern cultures, especially Indian, Moslem, and Chinese, all of which are largely ignored by Western historians. L'Amour also refers repeatedly to the maps then possessed by sailors and navigators—maps ancient even in that day and age.

41. Les Dorr, Jr., "Fobos Phlops," *Final Frontier*, August 1989, p. 7.
42. Geneva Hagen, "Martian Mystery Strikes Again" [Newswatch section], *Caveat Emptor*, Fall 1989, pp. 33–34.
43. Wilford, "With Observer Silent, NASA Now Envisions 'Star Wars' Explorers of Mars," *New York Times*, August 27, 1993.
44. Wilford, "A Craft Nearing Mars Sends Back Only Silence," *New York Times*, August 25, 1993, pp. A1, A11.
45. Gary Taylor, "Fir$t Things Fir$t," *Final Frontier*, April 1989, pp. 12, 13.
46. Steven A. Holmes, "Russia, U.S. Sign Space, Energy Deal," *Patriot News*, Harrisburg, PA [*New York Times* News Service, September 2, 1993], p. A6.

Chapter Six:

A Gathering

The Arizona sun was hot, the temperature over one hundred degrees, and I luxuriated in the absence of humidity.

A mile away, the Superstition Mountains rose at the end of a long, hard-packed dirt road. They stood tall and angular, unlike the ancient, worn Appalachians of my native Pennsylvania. I focused my camera, shifted position and shot several frames. Then I turned and hiked back to where I had parked the rental car.

I was in Arizona on vacation. I was also there to attend a gathering of UFO investigators and enthusiasts: the 26th Annual National UFO & New Age Conference, co-sponsored by ufologist Timothy Green Beckley and Jim Speiser, founder and former director of ParaNet, a UFO computer information service.

My plan had been to arrive in Phoenix, the conference site, two days early. I would tour the old Apache Trail (U.S. 88) one day and run south to Nogales, Mexico the next.

An airline cancellation put me in Phoenix much later than expected; I was forced to postpone my visit to Mexico. I did spend a full day following the Apache Trail—stopping frequently to hike in the desert, and grabbing a burger and beer in tiny Tortilla Flat (pop. 6). By day's end I was back in Phoenix, and the next day the conference began.

My recollection of the conference, held in September 1989, is included here solely as a personal account of the people, the mood, and one or two rather unusual experiences.

Thursday night, September 14, I was enjoying dinner alone in the restaurant of the Quality Inn West, the site of the conference. Occasionally, as I dined, a young woman working in the adjacent lounge would walk through the dining room on the way to the kitchen. Each time she opened the heavy lounge door, a roar of conversation could be heard. Finishing my meal, I asked the girl—her name was Linda—if the noise in the lounge was caused by persons registered for the conference. She said it was, and added that her lounge was "usually not this noisy."

Walking around to the main entrance, I was able to look in and study the crowd without being seen. Seated at a table was James W. Moseley, one of the most recognized persons in ufology today. And he should be: he was investigating UFOs when they were still called "flying saucers," and organized the first large-scale convention devoted to the subject. Currently he edits the irreverent *Saucer Smear*, a humorous, opinionated insider's periodical available free—provided you are on Jim's mailing list and post him an occasional letter.

Surrounding Moseley were several people, some familiar, some not. Tim Beckley—conference co-host and publisher of New Age and UFO books[47]—was on his feet, moving restlessly around the room. Though we had never met, I recognized him from published photos. Also moving about was Antonio Huneeus, another man I had never met. Antonio divides his time between writing activities in New York City and UFO research in his native Chile. Seated opposite Jim was a face not immediately identifiable, though familiar. It turned out to be Edward Biebel, formerly of Cleveland and now living in Nogales, Arizona. Ed is a longtime ufologist and a professional photographer. Still another seated with Moseley was Jim Speiser, though I had no idea who he was until we were introduced.

Watching Moseley from across the lounge, I recalled my first contact with the man in more than a decade. A year earlier I had written to Jim at the urging of UFO researcher Floyd Murray. In my letter, I asked to be added to Jim's mailing list. Moseley quickly responded—dubbing me "Agent Orange" in his reply. It was a joke based on the paranoia that has always clouded the UFO field. Everyone suspects everyone else of being a government spy. I currently work for the government, though in a rather lowly position and not, of course, as a spy, but Jim couldn't resist the inference.

I turned it around on him when I walked into the lounge. "Sir," I said, looking directly at Moseley. "Agent Orange, reporting as ordered."

The conversation at the table fell off noticeably. Moseley sat there, his mouth hanging open. He stared at me. Then he looked around at everyone else. "Who is this guy?" he finally asked. No one replied. "Does anyone know who he is?"

No one did. I had changed in twelve years. Finally, I told them, but Jim didn't understand the Agent Orange reference. I reminded him about his note. He didn't remember.

A moment later I was seated with the group, sparring verbally with Moseley and Biebel. The banter was good-natured and jovial. Watching Beckley, I sensed his preoccupation, his need to make the conference a success. Speiser, on the other hand, impressed me with his relaxed, quiet attitude—though he missed little of what went on around him. At one point I looked up as author Brad Steiger entered the lounge. I rose and introduced myself. Someone else—Moseley, I think—muttered "Broad Stagger" (recalling a published article satirizing the man).

Brad and I corresponded during the 1970s, but we had never previously met. He remembered my name and accepted a handshake. He had a strong grip, an easy smile, and radiated tremendous good will.

The conversation continued into the wee hours. Finally, Linda threw us out of the lounge.

Despite the late night, I was up early the following morning. I exercised and showered, and was off to the restaurant for breakfast. There I was hailed from a side table where Ed Biebel was seated with several others.

The breakfast conversation focused in part on UFO matters, though none of it seriously. In fact, the previous night's conversation had waxed serious only once: that was when Brad, Ed, and I touched on some unpleasant moments in the field—events that included, for each of us, strange and sometimes frightening phone calls or telephonic interference, or phenomena such as the automobile headlight problem described in the Foreword. Such phenomena are mysterious, and they are an intrinsic part of the UFO experience. They generate fear and paranoia, and serve only to intensify any involvement with the unknown.

Later that morning, a press conference was held to preview scheduled talks. Unfortunately, most speakers saw fit to roll through vast portions of their planned presentation. Instead of whetting the media appetite, they killed it. The one camera crew present packed up long before the list of speakers was exhausted. Eventually, the only people on hand represented the UFO/New Age fields.

Gene Steinberg made his first weekend appearance during the press gathering. I have known Gene for many years. A sometime publisher, he was pivotal in my development as a writer. In the early 1970s, while working as a professional radio newsman, he launched a magazine called *Caveat Emptor*,[48] focusing on reports of UFOs and unexplained phenomena. Floyd Murray and I became two of Gene's regular contributors. We were both novices—wannabes in the world of journalism. Gene gave each of us a voice in his magazine.

Gene and I had last been at a convention together fourteen years earlier, in October 1975, at the Trade Winds Inn, Fort Smith, Arkansas. The event was billed as the first International UFO Conference and attracted a plethora of players, including a large number of scientists and engineers as well as representatives of every large UFO research group. It was supposed to be a program "united for objectivity," but tension and antagonism were evident throughout—so much so that physicist Stanton Friedman, a guest speaker and no stranger to the controversy that abounds in UFO circles, declared of the group hostilities: "A pox on all their houses if they wish to fight with one another."

Indeed, those who paid admission to hear more about the UFO phenomenon found the atmosphere repellent. Allen Greenfield of Atlanta, Georgia, a ufologist and one of the brightest thinkers in the field, summed up the disgust many felt for the petty rivalry: "I'm picking up vibes of discontent from all over," he said. "They're getting sick of it."

Like many UFO conventions, the Fort Smith conference was more of a reunion of old friends and enemies than a platform for scientific endeavor. That it succeeded in attracting a number of scientists was a step in the right direction, but Gene and I were there merely to report and enjoy, and we did, though sometimes we too got caught in the arguments.

Gene was vacationing with his wife and son in nearby Scottsdale at the time of the 1989 Phoenix gathering. Because of this, he found himself traveling to and fro, dividing his time between family and conference. Subsequently, he missed a few of the more unusual events, none of which were on any scheduled agenda.

For reasons not at all hard to understand, a substantial amount of shop talk (read: gossip) took place in the lounge of the Quality Inn. I entered that place Friday night to discover longtime ufologist Rick Hilberg of Cleveland, and his wife, Carol, seated at a table. They were accompanied by another woman who identified herself only as Suzanne.

Suzanne was a "contactee"—a person directly in touch with an alien intelligence. At least that was how she described herself. During a period of several hours, she related a long series of unusual—or extranormal—occurrences going back to her childhood. I won't go into detail, but suffice it to say that after lengthy discussion I was convinced Suzanne was telling the truth as she knew it. I was also convinced she was not a typical contactee—not merely passing along telepathic messages from "space brothers."

Rather, her experiences were much broader, much more involved. These included out-of-body phenomena, psychic phenomena, contact with non-corporeal (energy) entities, and brief, actual, clinical death. That Suzanne embodied (or hosted) a tremendous power I have no doubt. During the course of our conversation she watched me carefully, and several times unnerved me with direct, piercing comments about my life, my past.

At one point she said, "You hold your pain close to you. You won't let it go." In that simple observation, prompted by nothing else in our dialogue, she touched all the agony, self-recrimination, and doubt I was embracing as a result of an emotionally wracking episode several years before. A few minutes later she disclosed her birthday—identical to my own: July 12.

This was nothing compared to what happened next. We were talking, surrounded by the sounds of the lounge—laughter, loud debate, pool balls clacking and falling. Without warning, Suzanne shifted to a kind of chant, or mantra. This penetrated the din, pulsing into my awareness.

I am not an easy subject for hypnosis. Professionals have found in me strong resistance to this state, and my efforts to employ auto-suggestive methods have had limited success, but within seconds I was slipping. I was locked to the cycle of her words—which she later described as a "now" affirmation. Abruptly, she broke the contact. Feeling dazed, I asked what that was all about. Suzanne laughed, offered a vague reply, and turned the conversation elsewhere. Then she did it again—a sledgehammer aimed at the psyche.

To say such an experience is unnerving is to greatly understate the issue. Still, I found myself enjoying Suzanne's company. When the lounge closed for the night, she decided to remain overnight rather than drive home. (She said she had not registered in advance for the conference, but attended spontaneously in order to try to meet other contactees or psychic channelers.)

Unfortunately, the inn was already filled; no rooms were available. A LaQuinta Inn was located directly across the highway. I suggested she try there, and escorted her to that establishment. There, as she registered, an odd bit of synchronicity surfaced.

Several times during the evening Suzanne had used the expression "I grok"—a phrase (roughly equivalent to "I understand") coined by the late science fiction writer Robert Heinlein in his novel *Stranger in a Strange Land*. I recall telling her that I had not heard that expression in many years.

While standing in the lobby of the LaQuinta, watching the desk clerk complete Suzanne's registration, I noticed a tired, worn paperback lying open on the lobby desk. The clerk was reading a copy of Heinlein's book.

After seeing Suzanne to her room, I returned to my own and immediately fell asleep. In fact, I slept somewhat longer than I had planned.

At breakfast Saturday morning, I found myself seated with a young man I'll call John. He had traveled from the Midwest to the conference hoping to find help with contactee-type problems of his own. Again, I'll not go into detail. I will say, though, that John was greatly troubled. He appeared exhausted—as though he had not slept soundly in a week.

As I listened to his story, we were joined briefly by Gene Steinberg, and a short time later by Suzanne. As I introduced her to John, I hoped she might be able to help ease his state of mind. She listened as he again told his tale and then she quietly directed the conversation elsewhere. Later, I asked Suzanne why she failed to respond to John's story. She replied that any sharing of his experience would cause him to remain focused on his own unhappiness, thereby magnifying the problem. The only way to truly help, she said, was to direct his attention to something more positive and pleasant. This sounded plausible, so I let the subject drop, but it continued to nag at me.

Not until I was on the airplane, en route to Pennsylvania on the following day, did I finally recognize why Suzanne's response bothered me. I have been taught that if you can offer someone kindness, do it. If you can offer help, even if only in the most elementary way, then do so. To ignore, or fail to respond to, another's pain is simply to divorce oneself from humanity. Suzanne did not ignore John's plea for help, but her effort to redirect his focus certainly left him believing that she did. Thinking about this on the airplane, I concluded that her way of helping was no help at all—only another way to avoid getting involved.

I was with Suzanne again on Saturday afternoon, having met up with her following a rather long presentation. Outside the lecture hall, we came upon Brad Steiger. I introduced the two only to discover that she and Brad were already acquainted.

Suzanne explained that she had been traveling one night when something "guided" her to a particular home in Scottsdale. When she rang the doorbell, Brad answered. Her verbal reaction at the time, she said, was something like: "I don't know who lives here or why I'm here, but I guess I'm supposed to be here." Brad, who was entertaining guests, invited Suzanne to join them.

Brad later admitted that the encounter pretty much happened the way Suzanne described it. When I told him about the disturbing power she demonstrated the previous night, he frowned thoughtfully and nodded. "Yes," he said, "there is a strange energy surrounding her."

Still later in the afternoon I was again in the lounge, involved in a conversation with Jim Vincent and Keith Michaels, editors of *Oddysey* (an intentional misspelling), a UFO research newsletter. Both men are young, and when we were joined by Rick Hilberg, we spanned a generation of UFO study.

I was acutely aware, during that talk—as I think was Rick—of how much time had passed since he and I were last active in ufology. I had discussed this with Gene Steinberg, who put it into words: "When we got involved," Gene said, "we learned from people like Moseley, [the late writer/researcher] Gray Barker, and [John] Keel; they were older, they had the experience. Now we're among the old-timers. Maybe it is our turn to be the teachers."

Maybe. But then maybe not.

My own view of the younger men and women at the conference—the newcomers to the field such as Vincent and Michaels—is that they are bright and capable. If there is any lack on their part, it is a tendency to disregard most views in ufology except those focusing on the extraterrestrial hypothesis—the insistence that UFOs are alien spacecraft. This is an old dogma, present for nearly fifty years in this country, and almost no one in the UFO community has escaped its influence. Unfortunately, efforts to prove the ET hypothesis appear to be going nowhere—accounts of "crashed discs" and dead aliens notwithstanding.

There is, and has always been, reason to believe that the UFO phenomenon is representative of something much more complex than spacecraft and visiting extraterrestrials. This leads into areas of religion, philosophy, and metaphysics—the combination of which can leave a lasting, and disturbing, impression on the human psyche.

Frankly, I must admit that the ET hypothesis is a more attractive (or at least more easily understood) alternative. Furthermore, I am not saying that the ET concept is wrong, only that it represents—for me, at least—too limited a view based on far too little information.

Saturday night was a banquet night, with Brad Steiger and his wife, Sherry, serving as guest speakers. I found myself at a table with the Hilbergs, Ed Biebel and his friend Mary from Tucson, and several others. As I looked around at the assembly, I noticed Suzanne seated off to one side with a number of women who all seemed to be paying her close attention. She must have noticed my gaze for she abruptly looked up and smiled. As the meal commenced, the conversation at my table escalated nicely, ranging from *Star Trek*, to Native American philosophy, to views on our troubled planetary environment. I was repeatedly surprised at the depth of concern evident whenever we touched on environmental issues, but I should not have been: whatever their personal or professional differences, the members of the UFO community are nonetheless a fairly sensitive, issue-oriented group—far more so, I believe, than has ever been acknowledged by the popular media, or by the community itself. This view was upheld by the message in Sherry Steiger's softly delivered address—a message of hope, love, global awareness, and environmental concern.

Following the banquet, I walked outside and sat on the sidewalk in front of the lobby. I felt tremendously relaxed and at peace. As I sat there, a woman approached and asked if I knew Suzanne's whereabouts. I recognized her as one of those who had been seated with Suzanne inside. She admitted to having been captivated by the woman's energy and charisma, and urgently wanted to speak with her again; but Suzanne was gone—vanished into the night without a word to her newfound friends.

About 1:00 A.M., Sunday, Moseley and Beckley assembled a group outside at the swimming pool, ostensibly to review the conference so that proposed future conventions might be better organized. At that point I realized something was absent: the bickering and strife I normally associated with such gatherings had been missing all along.

It was a welcome, refreshing absence.

NOTES
47. Inner Light Publications, New Brunswick, NJ.
48. *Caveat Emptor* was first published by Gene Steinberg in autumn 1971, and ran fifteen issues before being discontinued. The magazine was resurrected in late 1988 for an eight-issue run—until the fall of 1990—before again being discontinued by Steinberg.

In the Fields and Forests

An almost infinite variety of known and unknown creatures thrive on this mudball and appear regularly year after year, century after century.

–John A. Keel

Chapter Seven:

The "Thing" of Sheep's Hill

The creature was described in various ways: some said it was a panther, others said a wild dog, a black fox, or even a bear. Whatever it was, in 1945 it thoroughly unnerved the residents of Pottstown, Pennsylvania, by stealing poultry, screaming deep into the night, and making twenty-foot leaps to avoid gunfire.

Then, after a week of nocturnal activity, the creature vanished. Twenty-eight years later it—or something like it—returned to nearly the same location.

The story of the mystery animal of 1945—known as "the thing of Sheep's Hill"—came my way through a strange kind of luck, or synchronicity. While searching the microfilm files of a newspaper "morgue" for something else entirely, I happened across a short news item about the animal. I might have paid it little notice were it not for the fact that at the time, in March 1973, yet another "creature" was being reported in the vicinity of Pottstown.

Observed briefly and not very clearly by most witnesses, the 1973 animal was a screaming nighttime shadow with "piercing red eyes" and an odor like sulfur or rotten eggs.[49] Frightening and repugnant, it was also dangerous—systematically raiding the local poultry pens and causing such an uproar that armed search parties were organized to comb the woods of Upper Pottsgrove Township. The creature proved as elusive as smoke. In the end, all that came of the search efforts was that several posse members managed to get shot.

The episode of November 1945 appears to have been much the same. A creature or animal of some kind began appearing in a wooded area known as Sheep's Hill in the township of North Coventry. For a week it stayed in the area while moving mainly at night, eluding all efforts by search parties. During this period chickens began to disappear, and the creature was blamed. Descriptions varied greatly, but many witnesses reported that the animal screamed "like a baby" or voiced "a shrill cry." A few people claimed to see it move in bounds that covered ten to twenty feet.

A number of casualties occurred, all indirectly related to the presence of the beast. Quoting from an Associated Press story dated November 14, 1945:

> Police reported William J. Brandel, an 18-year-old Pottstown youth, was struck in the thigh by a "pumpkin ball" bullet [a lead slug fired from a shotgun]; Betty Hart, 17, of nearby Douglassville, was injured in the left arm by a "trigger nervous" posse member, and a young couple—tracking the "thing" by auto—were seriously injured when a frightful screech caused the driver to lose control of the car.

A Montgomery County farmer, identified as John Hipple, told reporters he saw the creature close up, and "it was like a big cat. I shot at it," he said, "and it leaped twenty feet into the air and, screaming, disappeared." Another witness, John Wojack of Pottstown, said the beast "gave a shrill cry then it bounded away in leaps of at least ten feet in length each."

A week after discovering the 1945 news story, I sat down with an almanac and played out a hunch. Studying a map showing the zoning of townships in the Pottstown area, I found that the two series of events—though separated in time by almost twenty-eight years—had occurred in virtually *the same location*. All of the sightings took place within roughly a five-mile radius, overlapping the common border of the municipalities of Upper Pottsgrove and North Coventry. That it could happen twice in the same place is both unlikely and uncanny, and not at all easy to dismiss. As for the animal itself: the most prosaic explanation is that, in each case, the creature was a puma.

Known also as cougar or mountain lion (*Felis concolor*), the puma can project an amazing variety of sounds—anything from bird-like chirps to blood-curdling cries. What's more, the animal can elude most forms of pursuit and easily leap twenty feet or more, but pumas are officially extinct in Pennsylvania (a notion we'll examine closely in the next chapter). They are not supposed to be black, as the Pottstown animals apparently were, nor do they possess an odor even vaguely like sulfur, or have red eyes. Furthermore, wild pumas tend to shy from man. For a big cat to remain near a human community, especially when it is being hunted, runs completely contrary to its instinct for survival.

Viewed in this light, the puma explanation hardly holds up, and it would seem something else entirely is responsible for episodes such as those at Sheep's Hill.

When the Europeans began colonizing North America in the seventeenth century, they brought with them a good deal of emotional and psychological baggage—including a very primal "fear of the beast." Barely suppressed in the best of times and by the most "civilized" of men, this fear is drawn from a time when wild predators occasionally dined on our terrified, early ancestors.

So imagine the consternation of the newcomers when they found their age-old enemy the wolf quite at home on these shores. Even worse, other large predators were here as well—among them the puma and grizzly bear—and the colonists set about destroying them with all available means. In the end the beasts had no chance—their animal cunning no match for man's driven nature, his adaptability and intelligence.

Today men are less bloodthirsty—less anxious to exterminate the beasts of the land. The upright, hair-less monkey with the opposable thumbs is discovering that there is great value in diversity of life: that all indigenous creatures, including the large, wild predators, have a right to survive, and without the mix there is no balance on this planet.

However, not everything that moves and breathes seems always a part of our world. There are beasts that appear but briefly. They cause mischief and may-hem and leave physical impressions such as hair, feces, or footprints—spoor that usually proves untraceable and seldom matches anything known. They are often of a recognizable form, like a cat or a dog, though they are always somehow different—in color, perhaps, or size. They seem immune to gunfire, have the ability to vanish without trace, and when confronted by man occasionally demonstrate a level of intelligence that goes beyond animal cunning.

* * *

In the fall of 1971, two years before events recurred in Pottstown, residents of Fairfax County, Virginia, entertained a series of visitors that ranged from the merely bizarre to the truly terrifying. First, a costumed character known as "Bunny Man" ran amok, threatening residents with an axe.

Later, a man dressed in a Superman costume dropped in on a meeting of the local board of directors. After offering some appropriately heroic words he departed as quickly as he had come, leaving the directors sitting there slack-jawed. The local media reported these events as Halloween fluff, but on November 3, 1971, a far more serious train of events was set into motion.

That night, residents of the Fort Belvoir, Virginia, area began reporting the disappearance of their dogs. One of these animals was a German shepherd. In the dense forest surrounding the Army installation, unearthly screams and moans were heard. Then, on the following night, a soldier identified as Lonny Davis witnessed the near end of his mongrel—a beagle-sized dog named One-Eye.

In his home on the outskirts of the installation, Davis heard his dog yelping in terror outside. Grabbing a flashlight, he dashed to his back door and yanked it open. Again he heard a yelp and to his right he noticed a large, dark shape loping toward the forest. The dark shape, he later declared, was carrying his dog in its mouth.

Acting on impulse and adrenaline, the soldier set out in pursuit, waving his flashlight and yelling at the top of his lungs. Perhaps startled by the screaming pursuer, the mystery animal dropped the dog and fled into the timber. Gathering up the injured One-Eye, Davis drove to the veterinary clinic at Fort

Belvoir, where the dog was treated for tooth punctures of the chest and rib cage. According to the vet, the dog-snatcher was no small animal—the punctures from its fangs were an inch deep.

In the following days, residents of the area scoured the woods looking for some sign of the mystery creature. Tracks were found: palm-sized prints that looked like cat tracks except they showed claw marks—a trait uncharacteristic of cats.[50] Traps were set and baited with deer meat, but to no avail. In the District of Columbia, experts were called upon to identify the tracks, which were plaster-cast. The prevailing opinion was that the prints were those of a puma, but no one could explain the claw marks.

At the time of these occurrences I was a member of the military, assigned to nearby Andrews Air Force Base in Maryland. Having read newspaper accounts of the dog-snatcher and the cat-like tracks, I drove to the Fort Belvoir area hoping to speak with Davis. The man was not at home, nor was he available on a subsequent visit. A nearby gas station attendant added a detail not published in any newspaper. On the night of November 4—the same night the creature grabbed Davis's dog—the attendant said he'd just turned off the outside floodlights prior to locking up when someone knocked at the door. The time was about 10:00 P.M.

When he opened the door, two state troopers entered and asked to purchase cigarettes. They seemed edgy, the attendant explained, and when he asked if there was trouble one of the pair replied they were investigating reports of a "big cat" down the road. The troopers didn't, or wouldn't, go into detail and departed as soon as they paid for their cigarettes. In retrospect it is clear they were investigating the incident at the Davis home.

Several weeks later, I spoke with a forest ranger in Virginia's Shenandoah National Park (the famous Sky-Line Drive). Curiosity caused me to ask about puma reports in the state. The ranger replied that twenty-five years had passed since there had been an authentic report of a lion in the Virginia mountains.

In 1977, a large dark animal resembling a puma began killing sheep in Allen County, Ohio. Loren Coleman, a cryptozoologist who has devoted considerable time to investigating such reports, compiled a detailed account of the killings for the November 1977 issue of *Fate*.[51]

A good deal of publicity surrounded the sheep killings, which began in March 1977 and continued until late May of that year. The killings were largely confined to Richland Township, with the attacks occurring on at least three separate farms. A principal player in this drama was William Reeder, dog warden and executive director of the Allen County Humane Society.

Coleman reported that Reeder had been working long hours investigating attacks on domestic livestock and poultry at the various farms. During a three-month period, more than one hundred sheep, several ducks, some peacocks, and a German shepherd were killed, and a good many more animals injured.

On at least one farm the sheep were savaged: clawed and bitten extensively and wantonly, the killer clawing apart a gate to get at the penned animals. While some sheep survived initially, most of the survivors later died of their injuries. Tracks found during the period were similar to those found in Fairfax County, Virginia—large and cat-like but showing non-retractable claws. Feces "the size of silver dollars" were found by Reeder, who had the samples analyzed by veterinarians in Lima, Ohio. The feces, according to Coleman (who interviewed Reeder), "were found to contain balls of hair and hookworms—all characteristic of cat scat." On the morning of May 27, 1977, events reached a startling climax for Reeder who, along with two police officers and a sheriff's deputy, managed to corner the suspected livestock killer in a plowed field near the town of Lafayette. The creature was described by Reeder as black, between one and one-half and two feet tall and having "the pointed ears of a cat." In his *Fate* article, Coleman describes Reeder's experience as follows:

> It was 2:00 A.M. ... and Reeder, an off-duty sheriff's deputy and two Lafayette police officers were using large flashlights and spotlights. The deputy circled around in the nearby woods. They all had a pretty good view of the animal and slowly began walking toward the cat. When they were within thirty-five yards of it the cat calmly began to walk toward them "like it was going to be a docile animal," Reeder said. But when it was only about twenty yards away, "within tranquilizer gun range," all of a sudden it broke for the woods.

Reeder told Coleman that the animal dashed 150 yards to the woods, where it was sighted by the deputy sheriff before vanishing into the timber. Tracks found at the scene were exactly like those found at other locations in the region—large and cat-like, but showing visible claw marks. More interesting, however, were the actions of the cat, which demonstrated a surprising intelligence—almost as if the animal knew it could easily elude its human pursuers.

In July 1986, in the small northeastern Pennsylvania town of Nicholson, Police Chief Leonard Schwartz was eating breakfast in the Bridgeview Diner when he was interrupted by a man who claimed to have seen a tiger. "He saw it at 6:00 A.M. and said it ran from some bushes in front of him and then turned around and ran back. He was only about fifty feet away from it," Schwartz told the Associated Press.

Although he expected to be laughed at, Schwartz notified state police. Instead, troopers from the Gibson barracks in Susquehanna County turned out in force, armed with rifles and a helicopter. They began searching the border of Wyoming and Susquehanna counties, where Carl Eastwood, a retired handyman, had reported seeing the animal.

"As far as I could see, it was a tiger," Eastwood told reporter Dan Meyers of the *Philadelphia Inquirer*.[52] He described it as large, about 350 pounds, and brown with white spots. "It frightened me," he said.

Eastwood reported the sighting on July 27, 1986. The following day a police dispatcher told reporters the animal had been spotted by the crew of a National Guard helicopter. He said the crewmen described it as a small tiger weighing about two hundred to three hundred pounds. The animal was quickly lost to view in dense woodland.

A Newton, Pennsylvania, school teacher, Gary Steier, along with his wife and son, reported seeing a tiger-like cat on a woodland trail near their home. "It was really big," Steier told Dan Meyers.[53] "It ran like a tiger you see on TV, long and loping." Steier, however, said the animal was orange in color.

In fact, descriptions of the cat's pelage varied greatly—from beige to orange to white, with either stripes or spots—causing considerable skepticism in some quarters. George Lowry, director of the Nay Aug Park Zoo in Scranton, Pennsylvania, observed:

"There is no cat I know of that weighs 350 pounds with white spots."

Meanwhile, police tried trapping the animal using the carcass of a whitetail deer as bait. The tiger never showed. Nervousness began to develop among local residents and state troopers were ordered to shoot to kill if the animal surfaced. The order to destroy the cat may have prompted a series of anonymous calls received by the Susquehanna County Humane Society in Montrose, Pennsylvania. The caller, who pleaded that the animal be spared, claimed it was a white Bengal tiger owned by a Nicholson man. The caller also said the animal had escaped from the owner's apartment while he was out hunting for a new home for it. Police themselves speculated that the cat escaped from a circus or wildlife menagerie, but no one came forward to claim ownership of the animal. After two full days and no further sightings, the search was ended for the mystery tiger of Nicholson.

Large cats are not the only animals to mysteriously appear, elude searchers, and disappear. Sometimes the creatures are huge terrifying dogs.

The dog reports, on the whole, seem less prevalent than accounts of mystery cats or "phantom panthers," as Loren Coleman prefers to call them. Nonetheless they are widespread enough—occurring in many lands and countries. Great Britain especially has a history of what researchers in that country call the "black dog" phenomenon, and the stories go back generations. America, too, has its "black dog" stories, such as the following report from May 1976.

According to various news accounts of the time, a Philip Kane of Abington, Massachusetts, was awakened on May 2, 1976, by his daughter, who insisted he check on the condition of her two ponies tethered in the back yard. The time was about 7:00 A.M. Kane reportedly was stunned to find the ponies lying on their sides, their halters tangled—their throats torn open. Hovering over one of the carcasses, eating from it, was a huge black and brown dog.

Kane told reporters that perhaps it was his fright, but the dog seemed quite huge—at least as large as the Shetland pony over which it was standing! Otherwise it looked something like a mix of Doberman and German shepherd. Somehow, despite his fear, he managed to chase the monstrous dog, which vanished into the nearby timbered bottomland.

A week of police searches failed to turn up the killer dog, even though others living in the area continued to report it, or something like it. One account had the dog crossing a street in full daylight—with blood dripping from its jaws!

NOTES
49. Glowing red eyes and an odor like sulfur or rotten eggs are characteristics cited often in old-world stories of demons and were-beasts.
50. There are four species of wild cat in North America: the jaguar, puma, lynx, and bobcat. The jaguar, the largest of the four, was once fairly abundant in the Southwest and in some areas of the South, such as Louisiana, though it is now seldom found north of Mexico. The puma is second in size to the jaguar and its distribution is widespread throughout the West, particularly California. The lynx is found throughout Canada with some overlap into the United States. The bobcat has the widest distribution of the four—

found in nearly the entire United States, Mexico, and in southern Canada where it overlaps with the lynx. All of these cats have retractable claws which are sheathed when they walk; their tracks do not show claw marks.

51. Loren Coleman, "Phantom Panther on the Prowl," *Fate*, November 1977, pp. 62–67. Also documented in *Creatures of the Outer Edge*, by Jerome Clark and Loren Coleman (New York: Warner Books, 1978), pp. 209–217; and referenced in Coleman's *Mysterious America* (Boston: Faber and Faber, Inc., 1983).

52. Dan Meyers, "The Upstate Tiger: More Sightings, Fear—And Doubts," *Philadelphia Inquirer*, July 29, 1986, p. 1A.

53. Ibid.

Chapter Eight:

Return of the Eastern Puma

Phantom panther: an expression widely used by those who investigate reports of mysterious felids. Popularized by Loren Coleman and the Fortean researcher Jerome Clark, the phrase encapsulates the sort of anomalous cat activity recounted in the last chapter, but not all sightings of large cats are so inexplicable. Some are more prosaic. Simply put, sometimes the sightings are of mountain lions.

Found throughout America before being exterminated from much of its range, the mountain lion, or puma, has a lineage that goes back to the saber-toothed tiger of the upper Pleistocene. Popular literature would have us believe that early man killed off the saber-tooth, though environmental change probably hastened the end for that species of cat. There is, however, no guesswork regarding the plight of its descendant.

With the coming of the Europeans and the subsequent emergence of industrial civilization, the large, wild predators of North America fell under constant attack. In the United States, bounties were placed on the gray wolf and the puma, and both species were relentlessly hunted, poisoned, and trapped.

Today the wolf still faces adversity, while thanks to stringent hunting laws the puma has made a comeback in the American West. In the East, however, except for a remnant colony of some thirty animals in Florida, the cat is supposed to be extinct. Reports outside of Florida are greeted with official skepticism and denial, but they occur nonetheless. Investigation is left to the cryptozoologists, who study accounts of unknown or anomalous animals. In one documented case, puma sightings were accompanied by tracks, which were cast; in another, a television news camera operator, videotaping an interview with a witness, obtained footage of an animal that looked like a cougar. What's more, of the literally hundreds of sightings reported each year in the East, a small percentage are of melanistic, or black-phase, pumas. Historically, the black puma does not exist in North America, though the animal has been found south of the equator.

Having spent a substantial amount of time following up on these reports, I'm convinced that at least some accounts are both legitimate and accurate. Recognizing the expanse of wilderness that remains in eastern North America, I'm further convinced that a few wild (as opposed to escaped) pumas survive largely undetected, though to get a proper perspective on this, one must first know something of the puma's history.

That the puma was once greatly abundant in the Western Hemisphere is evident from the stories and records handed down by early explorers, colonists, and hunters. Cristobal Colon, while on his fourth voyage along the coast of Nicaragua and Honduras in 1502, reported seeing *"leones"* (lions). William Penn knew of the puma in 1683. He described it as a creature "for profit only, by skin and fur, and which are natural to these parts ..." The comment was included in a 1933 volume, titled *Penn's Woods, 1682–1932*, by Edward E. Wildman. Captains Meriwether Lewis and William Clark, on their famed expedition, described an encounter with a puma along the Missouri River. The brief account was recorded by Lewis on May 16, 1805, two days after six of the expedition's best hunters, armed with muzzle loaders, wounded a grizzly and were in turn nearly killed by the bear before it succumbed to their collective gunfire.

Lewis wrote: "In the early part of the day, two of our men fired on a panther, a little below our encampment, and wounded it. They informed us that it was very large, had just killed a deer, partly devoured it, and was in the act of concealing the balance as they discovered him."

Daniel Boone is said to have witnessed a rare encounter between a puma and a bison. The incident was described by Timothy Flint in his 1856 *Life and Times of Colonel Daniel Boone*. Flint related how Boone and his brother were returning home in 1770 from their first exploration of Kentucky, when they came upon a stampeding herd. The bison were "in perfect fury," Flint wrote, "stamping the ground and tearing it up and rushing back and forward." The brothers soon saw the reason for the stampede. A puma was on the back of one of the larger bison, and had "fastened his claws into the flesh of the animal ... until the blood ran down on all sides."

Apparently upset by the puma's effort to kill the bison, Boone decided to try to unseat the cat with a long shot from his muzzle loader. "Picking the flint of his rifle and looking carefully at the loading," Flint said the frontiersman—famed for his marksmanship—took aim and hit the puma. "The panther released its hold and came to the ground," Flint related.

Philip Tome, who roamed the wilderness of northcentral Pennsylvania during the early 1800s, described the puma as "one of the most formidable animals encountered in the forests of this continent." The description appears in Tome's *Pioneer Life, or Thirty Years a Hunter*, a book originally published only a year before his death on April 30, 1855, and since republished by the Lycoming County (Pennsylvania) Genealogical Society.

In his lifetime, Tome became legendary as a hunter and a long-time interpreter for the chiefs Cornplanter and Blacksnake. His encounters with mountain lions were many, we are told, and in his book he observed that "the bear is the only animal that can cope with the panther. I once witnessed an encounter between a bear and a panther. From its superior agility the panther had the advantage at first, but when the bear became enraged by his wounds, he grasped his antagonist in his powerful paws, crushing and biting him to death almost instantly."

To say that the puma was regarded by the early settlers as something of a monster is no exaggeration. It was viewed as a creature of mystery, nearly supernatural in its ability to move undetected through the wilderness. James Pierce, writing his 1823 "Memoir on the Catskill Mountains," published by the *American Journal of Science and Arts*, described the puma as "an animal rarely seen; but from its strength, size, and ferocity it is regarded with terror, and considered to be the most formidable beast of the forest."

This dim view of the cougar was further encouraged by the often frightening cry of the cat; or perhaps more accurately, the various cries of the cat.

In 1893, Theodore Roosevelt described the sound of a prowling puma as "a loud, wailing scream ringing through the impenetrable gloom ..." Casper Whitney, writing of "The Cougar; Hunting In Many Lands," published in 1895 in the *Book of the Boone and Crockett Club*, said: "Their cry is as terror-striking as it is varied. I have heard them wail so you would swear an infant had been left out in the cold by its momma; I have heard them screech like a woman in distress; and again, growl after the conventional manner attributed to the monarch of the forest."

Still others have described the sound of the puma as a "queer, half-human cry;" or a "horrible, screaming cry." Such descriptions are not very flattering and no doubt did much to prompt extirpation of the cat in the East.

At the beginning of the 1800s, puma numbers were already greatly reduced in the East as hunting and trapping of the animal intensified.

In Pennsylvania, the last wild puma was said to have been killed during the 1870s, though there is some disagreement as to exactly where and when. The naturalist Helen McGinnis, who became well-known in wildlife circles for her study of the eastern coyote, reported in the February 1982 *Pennsylvania Game News* ("On The Trail of a Pennsylvania Cougar") that the last was believed shot in Berks County in 1874.

However, the naturalist Samuel N. Rhoads, in his 1903 *Mammals of Pennsylvania & New Jersey*, stated that he was unable to substantiate any accounts of Pennsylvania pumas killed after 1871. Rhoads added that two unconfirmed kills were reported in Clinton and Clearfield counties in 1891.

Widely distributed in Pennsylvania, the puma was found in at least twenty-three counties. In neighboring New Jersey, the puma was found in most areas of the state, though the cat was believed extinct there by the early 1800s. In New York, the puma was also once abundant, especially in the Adirondacks. In 1871, a twenty dollar bounty was placed on the animal in that state. By 1882, a total of forty-six New York pumas had been reported killed in Essex, Franklin, Hamilton, Herkimer, Lewis, and St. Lawrence counties.

The cougar was reported extinct in most areas of New England by the early 1900s. In Vermont, the last wild puma was reported shot in 1881, though there are indications the cat was active in the state well into this century. In New Hampshire, where the puma was never greatly abundant, the cat was believed extinct by about 1852. However, on November 2, 1853, a cougar weighing 198 pounds and measuring eight feet, four inches (including tail) was said to have been shot in Lee Township, Rockingham County, New Hampshire.

In Virginia and portions of Maryland, the puma is believed to have been active in the 1880s, and in neighboring West Virginia until about 1915. But in these states, and in Pennsylvania, the reports continue even today.

In 1987, residents of the Ringtown–Zion Grove area in northern Schuylkill County, Pennsylvania, reported several encounters with a puma-like animal. One sighting was made the night of December 30 by Fred Ebert of Pattersonville.

According to an account in a local newspaper, Ebert had stepped outside to dispose of ashes and to check on his two dogs, which were barking wildly. At the same time, his male house cat, which had just emerged from the basement, did an about-face back into the cellar.

Looking in the direction indicated by the barking dogs, Ebert said he at first saw only a blur against the snow-covered ground, which was illuminated by bright moonlight. As his vision improved, he found himself watching a catlike animal he later estimated to be about three and one-half to four feet long.

Ebert described the animal as low to the ground, with a "long and curly" tail. Obtaining a flashlight, he backtracked its trail and discovered that it had wandered to within several feet of the house before being frightened by the dogs. Due to the softness of the snow, Ebert was unable to make positive identification of the tracks, but he added that tail-like drag marks were evident in several locations.

A sighting with multiple witnesses occurred in Berks County, Pennsylvania, during the fall of 1982. The witnesses were Kim Wampler of Pine Grove; her brother Lance of Bethel; and Justin and Dawn Beck, also of Bethel. The animal was sighted near Strausstown, Pennsylvania, along Route 183, while the four were spotlighting deer.

Recalling the incident, Lance said the spotlight illuminated a form which they at first believed to be a deer. A moment later it was evident they were watching a large cat—a bobcat, they all presumed.

Lance said someone produced binoculars and they began to glass the animal.

"We all got a good look at it," Lance said, "except maybe for Dawn. It was on the ground, near the edge of a pond." He described the cat as tan or light brown in color with a long tail. When it moved, "it slinked." The tail, he added, was perhaps half the length of the body.

"It was no bobcat," Lance declared. He said the animal was under observation for a full minute or two, "long enough for us to pass the binoculars around."

When veteran news reporter Wayne VanDine agreed to interview Ruth O'Brien about a cougar on her property, he did so, he said, "with mixed feelings." A reporter for KDKA–TV in Pittsburgh, Pennsylvania, VanDine recalled the events of June 1, 1982, during a long distance phone interview.

News accounts of the time indicate that O'Brien had been seeing and hearing a puma or pumas on her property for a number of years. One story in the *Pittsburgh Post Gazette*[54] said the occurrences went back to 1978, though at first O'Brien kept her knowledge secret for fear of ridicule.

VanDine said he was not expecting anything unusual to occur when he agreed to interview the woman. He was accompanied by several individuals. Among them were cameraman Ed Bailey, who lived near O'Brien's secluded home in Millerstown, Allegheny County; and James Hilderliter, president of Animal Protectors of the Allegheny Valley.

"The interview was under way and she [O'Brien] is telling me this story, and she's very convincing," VanDine related. "And then as we're wrapping things up, I'm looking around and I see this patch of brown in the grass some distance away that hadn't been there before. I'm a golfer, so I'm a fair judge of distance," VanDine declared, "and I had an unobstructed view. I'd say it was 120 yards away."

As he watched, VanDine said the "brown patch" stood up. "I looked around at the others and asked: 'Are you seeing what I'm seeing?'"

VanDine said Bailey began rolling videotape of the animal, which "to my eyes looked like a cougar." After a few seconds Bailey stopped the camera and began moving toward the creature. As he did, the animal moved off into the woods.

A couple of days later, VanDine made a trip to an area zoo to have a close look at a puma. He said he came away convinced that the animal on O'Brien's land was of the same species. Asked to describe the animal, VanDine said it was a solid brown or tan in color, catlike, and had a long tail. The animal was no bobcat, he said.

Hilderliter, during an interview in the *Alle-Kiski Valley News Dispatch*,[55] described the animal as having a long tail and a lean, sleek body. "This was definitely a cougar," he said.

As for the videotape, VanDine said it was broadcast along with the story, but unfortunately the distance from camera to subject was too great to allow much detail. He said KDKA technicians tried unsuccessfully to enlarge and enhance the videotaped image. Efforts to obtain still camera images from the videotape were only slightly more successful, with considerable detail lost in the process.

Two years later, in July 1984, large catlike tracks were discovered in South Buffalo Township—only a few miles from Ruth O'Brien's property.

The tracks were found in mud on the Alexander Lindsay farm by son Andy, who was driving a tractor. A plaster cast was made by Stan Gordon, of Greensburg, Westmoreland County. Until recently, Gordon—as head of the now defunct Pennsylvania Association for Study of the Unexplained—was an active investigator of eastern cougar reports, and had accumulated files on puma sightings in Pennsylvania going back to the 1940s. According to Gordon, the prints found on the Lindsay farm clearly were those of a puma. The plaster cast of the paw, he said, "is three and one-half inches wide, shows asymmetrical toes and a squared-off heel pad."

A photo of the cast was shown to naturalists Glenn and Danita Wampler of Lebanon County, Pennsylvania. For many years the Wamplers operated a wildlife menagerie, which included bobcats and cougars. Their cats were bred and distributed to zoos and menageries throughout the United States, and today their advice on caring for the big cats continues to be sought by other wildlife caretakers. The Wamplers still hold a valid menagerie license, though they now own but one cougar, a young female. After examining the photo, they agreed that it appears to be of a cast made from the track of a puma.

Earlier I mentioned that melanistic, or black-phase, cougars have been reported throughout the East, though such accounts are comparatively rare. Because black pumas are not supposed to occur north of the equator, wildlife management personnel pay scant attention to all such accounts in North America—ignoring the possibility that melanism among cougars may be widespread if not exactly common.

In Nova Scotia, Quebec, and New Brunswick, repeated daylight reports of black pumas have been largely discounted. In the eastern United States, such reports generate skepticism bordering on contempt.

One story difficult to dismiss comes from a woman living in a secluded area of Dauphin County, Pennsylvania: Esther Trough lives on a fifty-eight-acre wooded tract at the base of the Blue Mountains, east of Harrisburg. She resides in retirement with her husband, Jack, who was present during an interview that also included Danita Wampler. Recalling her experience, which occurred in 1983, Esther said the weather was warm and she had decided to go into the mountain in search of hemlock seedlings for her yard. Towing a small cart used to haul her plants, she set off along a quarter-mile path leading from her back yard to a small natural-spring reservoir.

"I was pulling this screechy little cart, looking down, when something dark passed in front of me," she recalled. "I looked up and there it was, and I thought: Oh dear God, please don't let it jump on me."

Esther described the animal as puma-like with almond-shaped eyes and a "gorgeous, really long, thick tail." But the most striking feature was the cat's unblemished, solid black pelt—a trait of the melanistic puma as opposed to the jaguar, which shows faint spotting or discoloration even in the black phase.

For a brief, heart-skipping moment she said she stared at the cat, which stood on the far side of the small reservoir. The animal had apparently materialized from a high tree-shrouded shoulder immediately to the west of the pool. "I didn't know that it wouldn't jump," Esther said. "I didn't feel that it was hostile. It didn't snarl. I didn't even hear it, it was so quiet. I think it was surprised."

Taking control of her own surprise, Esther said she turned and walked at a fast but unhurried pace down the path. It was only when she was safely back in the house that a fear response set in and she began to shake.

Esther speculated that her "screechy cart" may have attracted the animal to what it believed was injured prey. (A walk into the area revealed the location to be thick with deer and other wildlife.) "It was magnificent," she said of the cat. "I could hardly take my eyes off it, but I knew I had to get back."

The encounter on the Trough property is not an isolated case. Over the years a number of individuals have admitted seeing large, puma-like animals in that portion of Dauphin County, as well as in neighboring Schuylkill and Lebanon counties. In one instance a bow hunter observed a big cat and described it as coal black.

Perhaps the most frequently heard argument against the existence of eastern United States pumas is that none has ever been killed by a hunter. (A small cougar was in fact killed in Crawford County, Pennsylvania, in 1967, but was believed reared in captivity.) Pumas travel alone, except for a female with kittens, and they shy instinctively from humans. Moreover, the expanse of wilderness to be found in the East, even today, is more than sufficient to hide a fairly large number of widely distributed, wide-ranging, cougars. The chances of a deer hunter during rifle season encountering a wild puma are probably one in ten thousand. A silent bow hunter would fare better.

Then again, even naturalists skilled in locating the cat don't always find their quarry. Edward A. Goldman, coauthor with Stanley P. Young of *The*

If You Like Strange Encounters …
You'll LOVE **FATE** Magazine!

Each month, FATE magazine brings you true reports of the strange, mysterious and unknown – spirit animals, guardian angels, UFOs and all things paranormal. Act now and save $51 – that's 60% off the newsstand price – when you subscribe to 24 issues of FATE. That's the same as getting one year for FREE! Or sign up for 12 issues for just $21.50 and save 49% off the cover price!

FATE

170 FUTURE WAY
PO BOX 1940
MARION, OH 43305-1940

Place
Stamp
Here

Puma: Mysterious American Cat (Dover Publications, 1946), noted that during a trip into Mexico he "traveled thousands of miles ... often camping in the main habitat of the animal, and seldom saw it."

Early American explorers also remarked on the elusive nature of the beast. Lewis and Clark, on their expedition, wrote that the puma "is very seldom found, and when found, so wary [that] it is difficult to reach him with a musket."

In 1982, the naturalist Helen McGinnis released a seventy-four-page document dealing with accounts of pumas in Pennsylvania since 1890. More than 290 individual sightings were included in the report. Her earlier study of the Eastern coyote (with John L. George, a professor of wildlife management at Penn State, where McGinnis had been a graduate student) attracted widespread attention and earned her a solid reputation. The cougar study received substantially less attention. She wrote, in summary:

> Plausible reports [of pumas] tend to cluster in specific regions, including a broad section of the north-central highlands as far east as southern Sullivan County; western Erie County; southern Forest, northern Jefferson and northern Clarion counties; southwestern Pennsylvania, including the outskirts of Pittsburgh; and west-central Schuylkill County and adjacent parts of Northumberland and Columbia counties. There were no reports from the southeastern corner of the state.[56] The distribution of reports is not obviously correlated with deer number, perhaps because they [deer] are generally abundant throughout the state, but does seem to be inversely proportional to human population density with some exceptions.
>
> I conclude that Pennsylvania presently supports a small, widely scattered population of wild cougars ... It is unlikely that [zoo or menagerie] escapees are involved in all or even most sightings ... because

reports tend to come from remote areas. If a majority were former captives, more would come from urban areas. Several accounts of two or more cougars together, including at least one of a mother with kittens, indicate the population is breeding.

Contrary to the opinion of at least one student of the eastern cougar, I suggest that a remnant population of cougars could survive in the northeastern states. The cougar is the ecological and behavioral equivalent of the leopard in the Old World. Leopards can survive without detection in heavily settled rural areas of Africa, and the elusive cougar has demonstrated that capability in California.

McGinnis noted that the average person's inability to identify the big cats or their sign properly, along with the popular opinion that they do not occur in the East, may be the true culprits behind the lack of hard evidence to substantiate their existence. In Pennsylvania, the best "evidence" to date is the television videotape of a big cat in Allegheny County in 1982, and the cast made from a track in Armstrong County two years later; but these bits of supporting data have done little to stir interest among wildlife officials. Stan Gordon, the researcher who obtained the cast of the cougar track, is of the opinion that Pennsylvania game management officials are beginning to demonstrate "a change in attitude" with regard to cougar reports. He said there may be concern within the state's game commission that if the puma is recognized, it would be relentlessly and unlawfully hunted. (Although officially extinct, the eastern puma is nonetheless protected under the federal Endangered Species Act.)

Dale Sheffer, director of the Pennsylvania Game Commission's Bureau of Game Management, said the agency has simply been unable to verify even one cougar sighting. "I don't personally feel there are any wild cougars breeding in the state," Sheffer said. But he added, "I feel it is possible for them to drift in, perhaps from West Virginia or some other state."

A few observations on puma habits and characteristics: Few people are truly aware of the tremendous speed and power of this big North American cat. Given the advantage of surprise, a puma can run down a deer (which can move at about thirty-five mph). It can also leap unbelievable distances. Jumps of twenty feet are commonplace; and a distance of forty or more feet is often within the cat's capabilities.

A few years ago I witnessed a demonstration of this jumping power. I was visiting the home of Glenn and Danita Wampler, the cougar experts mentioned previously. Also visiting was Jack Giles, a wildlife biologist and an expert on bobcats for the state of Pennsylvania.

Jack was preparing a classroom comparison of pumas and bobcats, and needed photos of puma tracks for his class. At one point he, Danita, and I entered an empty twenty-foot-long cougar kennel, where Jack proceeded to photograph paw prints in the soft earth. The cat normally housed in the kennel, a big male named Pepper, was temporarily confined to the adjoining kennel house. All that separated us from the cougar was a small door operated manually by a remote arm. The sounds issuing from the other side of that door clearly said Pepper was not happy.

Finally we exited and, as Jack closed and latched the outer gate, Danita threw the arm that opened the kennel house door. A heartbeat later Pepper crashed into the gate, yowling and spitting. The angry cat had effortlessly leaped the twenty-foot span of the kennel, and would have continued right past (or through!) us, had the gate not been closed.

While the puma's jumping power is astonishing, in matters of sheer brute strength the species is equally amazing. The well-known wildlife photographer, Leonard Lee Rue, III,[57] has reported that a western puma once dragged a horse weighing eight hundred to nine hundred pounds some thirty feet. The horse would have outweighed the cougar by at least six hundred or seven hundred pounds. Another is said to have carried an eight-month-old calf three miles up the face of a sheer mountain.

Captive pumas, Glenn Wampler has observed, require about twelve to fifteen pounds of meat a day. However, in the wild they will gorge themselves if the opportunity presents, eating as much as thirty pounds a day. When hungry, wild pumas are not finicky: "They certainly won't turn down a songbird, a chipmunk, a grouse, a woodchuck ... they'll eat whatever is available."

Average weight of an adult puma is 150 to 175 pounds, though a weight in excess of two hundred pounds is not extraordinary. The heaviest puma on record weighed 276 pounds after being eviscerated, and may have had a live weight of more than three hundred pounds, according to Leonard Rue.

Fully grown, the cats range from six and one-half to nine and one-half feet in length, including tail. The pelt color can vary greatly, depending on the climate and geographical location. Red, tan, brown, gray, black, and even white pelts have been reported.

The tracks of a puma (the word "puma," incidentally, comes from the Incas and means "lion") average three to four inches in width, though one cat, killed in the Sangre de Cristo Mountains of

Colorado in 1927, had a forefoot six and three-quarters inches wide.

Man and dogs are the puma's chief enemy, and for some reason the big cat fears dogs more than man. A puma will often tree at the sound of a pursuing pack, even though one swipe of a forepaw will generally put an end to the average dog.

The puma's only other natural enemy appears to be the jaguar. Where their territories overlap, in Mexico and a few areas of southern Arizona and New Mexico, the two have been known to clash. Though the jaguar is generally larger and stronger, it is said that the puma—our native North American lion—is most often victorious.

NOTES

54. Lisa Friedman, "Cougars Extinct Here? Maybe Not," *Pittsburgh Post–Gazette*, August 7, 1984, p. 5.
55. "Fawn Cat Makes Its TV Debut," *Valley News Dispatch* [Alle–Kiski Valley, Pennsylvania] June 2, 1982.
56. In 1982, when Helen McGinnis released her report on sightings of pumas in Pennsylvania, there were no known accounts from the southeastern corner of the state. However, for about a week in January 1995, literally dozens of people reported seeing a cougar in and around the Cobbs Creek Park area of Philadelphia. Among the witnesses were three police officers. The big cat was last spotted on January 25, after which it disappeared for good.
57. Leonard Lee Rue, III, *Complete Guide to Game Animals* (New York: Outdoor Life Books, 1981), p. 178.

Chapter Nine:

Bird Lore of the Black Forest

Enormous birds, larger than condors, once soared the skies over North America. This was long ago—thousands of years before Columbus, or Leif Eriksson. Fossil remains tell us these creatures were widespread across the continent. They also tell us that the great birds are extinct, or at least that's the prevailing opinion.

Is it possible, however, that a remnant population survived into colonial times? The indications are there, in legend and folklore. Even more startling is the possibility, albeit remote, that a few of the giant birds still exist—tottering on the brink of true extinction.

The American Indians spoke routinely of great birds which, they said, were a species unlike any other—not eagles or vultures, or even condors. They handed this lore down through the generations and across tribal groups so that by the time the Europeans arrived, the history of the great birds had acquired "a certain mythological content." Otherwise, according to the late zoologist Ivan T. Sanderson, it was "a perfectly straightforward statement of zoological fact."

"All that the Amerinds said," Sanderson observed, writing in the April 1972 issue of *Pursuit*,[58] "was that they had a truly giant condor that lived on mountain tops and was primarily nocturnal; and they had tens of thousands of wood and stone sculpts of this bird on their totem poles and other monuments out west."

These birds were known to the Native Americans by many names: *Heloha* to the Choctaw of the Southeast, *Tlanuwa* to the Cherokee, *Adee* to the Northwest Coast tribes, to list a few. European settlers came to know them as the thunderbirds—creatures so huge they were "monstrous."

Applied to contemporary reports of giant birds, that adjective has also been used as a proclamation of disbelief; nonetheless, they have been sighted time and again.

During the mid to late 1970s in southern Texas and Illinois, huge birds, or bird-like creatures, were reported by otherwise sensible residents. Rural and wilderness areas of New Jersey, Ohio, Kentucky, and West Virginia have all been the scene of encounters with giant birds. In Pennsylvania, the town of Jersey Shore was the focus of a wave of sporadic sightings that began about mid-1969 and continued until mid-1971.

Of course, anyone with brass enough to admit seeing such a bird is generally thought of as nearly ready for a padded cell. On the other hand, public ridicule doesn't always deter those who believe they have seen something unusual. Ask some of the older residents of the Allegheny Plateau, north of Jersey Shore. In this rugged wilderness region, and for more than one hundred years, the thunderbird has been an established part of local folklore.

Geologically, the Allegheny Plateau (also known as the Allegheny Highlands) is a two hundred-square-mile fold stretching from Harrisburg, Pennsylvania, north to Lake Ontario, New York. It is a region of abundant heavy timber, including the well-known Black Forest of Pennsylvania (primarily Potter and Clinton counties, with some overlap in Tioga and Lycoming counties to the east).

Several centuries ago the Black Forest was inhabited by the Susquehannock Indians, who for many years had been at war with their enemy to the north, the Iroquois.[59] By 1676 the Susquehannocks were defeated, and the Black Forest became the domain of the Iroquois and the Algonquin tribes to the east.

Rich in natural bounty, the Black Forest was jealously guarded by its residents, who forbade free exploration of the region by European settlers. Consequently, the territory became known as the Forbidden Land. By 1784, when the land was purchased under treaty, the locals were forced to give way.

One hundred years later, the booming lumber industry nearly eradicated this great American preserve. Millions of board feet of timber were felled and floated down the Susquehanna River to satisfy a growing nation's construction needs. By the early 1900s the industry had moved on, leaving parcels of barren land where entire forests once stood. Much of this land was later reforested by the Civilian Conservation Corps under the direction of President Franklin D. Roosevelt. Today these reforested areas, along with some three million acres of original woodland, form a wilderness that shelters comparatively few people and abundant wildlife. It is a place where a person could easily become lost, and where great birds could conceivably fly.

* * *

On a sunlit day in July 1987, Herb Nesman stood outside his summer residence in northwest Clinton County, and told of seeing a giant bird fly over an oil derrick he was working in 1978. Nesman's sighting—the last of many which he said dated to his childhood—occurred near the town of Snow Shoe in Centre County, some twenty miles south of the huge Alvin R. Bush Dam where his summer home was located.

"I was working for Delta Drilling," recalled Nesman, a cautious, alert man who once worked the western oil rigs, and whose manner of speech reflected a time spent in the West. "I was on the derrick, it was May or June, and I thought it was a small airplane until I saw its wings start flapping. Then I knew what it was."

What it was, in Nesman's understanding, was a California condor. He said he based this on stories he heard as a boy from a local historian and storyteller, the late Hiram R. Cramner.

"Hiram always said the birds were condors that had migrated east," Nesman explained. As a boy, growing up in the region, "it was nothing to see several [birds] at a time. When you saw them, it was always the wingspan that got you—they had such long wings. Now that I think about it, they weren't all the same size." Some, he said, "were monstrous, like adults and young birds flying together."

Asked to estimate the wingspan of the bird over Snow Shoe, Nesman was uncertain. "The derrick I was on was sixty or eighty feet high. The wingspan could have been over eighteen feet."

Nesman, who was operating a bait shop below Bush Dam, where huge birds have been reported in the past, said he never saw any of the creatures on or near the ground. He was therefore unable to offer details about head, claws, or body. He said the giant birds were more numerous years ago, when they were still occasionally seen in groups of two or three. "I think they're almost extinct," Nesman lamented, "if they aren't already."

Despite the lore handed down to Nesman and others by Hiram Cramner, these birds were almost certainly not condors. The nearly extinct California condor, *Gymnogyps californianus*, has a wingspan of about nine feet and is sooty black. Its South American cousin, the Andean condor, *Vultur gryphus*, has a span of ten to twelve feet and is glossy black with white upper wing coverts, and a collar of white neck feathers. These are the largest of known soaring birds, and yet, they are smaller than the elusive, wraith-like birds of the Allegheny Plateau, which are most often said to be gray to black in color.

But if not condors, what then? Imagination? So argued a highly skeptical representative of the Pennsylvania Game Commission—the agency charged with establishing and administering policy on wild game in the state. Or exaggerated reports of turkey vultures.

Another viewpoint came from long-time resident Charlie Cross in the mountains north of Bush Dam. "Maybe bald eagles," Cross said with a smile. He was seated in the living room of his home, with a storm rumbling outside. A lifelong outdoorsman and local wildlife expert, Cross seemed the ideal person to talk to about the legendary big birds of the Allegheny Plateau. Unfortunately, "I've never seen one. Personally, I think most of these [birds] are just stories," he declared with a grin.

In defense of this view, Cross explained that over the years he had worked variously as a lumberman and deputy forest ranger, a hunting guide and a trapper, and as a foreman for the old Civilian Conservation Corps. In 1986 he shot his sixty-second whitetail buck. "And in all that time I never saw any sign of a giant bird, and I used to walk thirty-five miles of trail and fourteen miles of line clearcut."

But Cross confirmed reports of a puma in the area, and he said bald eagles nesting near Bush Lake had been there for several years (a mature eagle was observed two days before the interview, flying over the lake). In fact, Cross suggested bald eagles as explanation for large birds spotted by Mr. and Mrs. Robert Lyman, Jr. of Coudersport, Potter County. However, this sighting—in 1973 near the village of Cross Fork, on the Clinton–Potter county border and ten miles from Bush Dam—was made years before anyone saw the eagles.

In a letter to the author,[60] Lyman said: "They [the big birds] are not like anything in our *Golden Field Guide to Birds of North America*. A calculation by trigonometry showed their wingspan at seven feet, maybe longer; they were not eagles or turkey vultures." During a subsequent telephone conversation, Lyman said he had revised his estimate to about twelve feet for each bird. Elaborating on the sighting, he said he was sitting on the porch of his family's hunting cabin with several friends "when we saw two very large birds ... directly across from the cabin." The birds were flying above a knoll and "I knew the elevation of that hill." Using a bit of mathematics and triangulation, he was able to arrive at his wingspan estimate.

Lyman's father, the late Robert R., Sr., scribed two books on unusual events in the Black Forest. His second volume, *Amazing Indeed*,[61] was published a

year before his death on April 2, 1974. It contains a
chapter devoted to local thunderbird lore, including
a sighting of his own. He wrote:

> About 1940, I saw a huge bird which I am certain was
> a thunderbird. It was on the ground in the center of
> Sheldon Road, about two miles north of Coudersport.
> It was brownish in color. Legs and neck were short. It
> was between three and four feet tall and stood upright
> like a very large vulture. When I was about 150 feet
> away it raised to fly. It was plain to see its wingspread
> was equal to the width of the road bed, which I mea-
> sured and found to be twenty-five feet. I will concede it
> may have been twenty feet but no less. The wings were
> very narrow, not over one foot wide. The bird ... could
> have gone straight up the road and missed the trees
> but it did no such thing. It flew off at right angles to
> the road, through dense second-growth timber and
> had no trouble.
>
> I gained the impression that this was a young
> bird, which may explain why I was able to get so
> close to it. Other local reports claim the thunder-
> birds are grayish in color. As they mature they may
> change from brown to gray.[62]

A historian and naturalist, with a degree in
forestry, Lyman made a thorough study of thunderbird
lore in the Black Forest. In doing so, he documented
many old reports, the earliest of which came from one
Elvira Ellis Coats.

Born in 1833, Elvira was the granddaughter of
Richard Ellis, founder of Ellisburg, Potter County. She
was said to have been acquainted with the Amerinds
who still lived there and who told her of huge birds
they often saw but never harmed. These birds were
described as vulture-like but much larger. When flying
they appeared enormous because of their wingspan!

Another early report was made by Fred Murray in 1892. A resident of Westfield, Tioga County, Murray claimed to have seen a flock of giant birds in Dent's Run, Elk County. He also described them as vulture-like but much larger, with a wingspan of at least sixteen feet.

According to Lyman: "The report made news at the time. An ornithologist from Pittsburgh came to Murray's lumber camp to observe them. He said similar birds had been seen in remote parts of West Virginia and Kentucky."

Yet another account dates to 1898, when a farmer near Centerville, Crawford County, supposedly live-trapped a huge bird that had been feeding on a dead cow. According to Lyman, the farmer managed to transfer the bird to a cage where it was viewed by A. P. Akeley, a superintendent of Potter County schools. Akeley is said to have described the bird as gray in color and over four feet tall, with short legs and neck.

"The farmer thought it was an Andean condor," Lyman reported. "Mr. Akeley says it was not black. There was no large white ruff of downy feathers around the lower part of the neck, and the skin above that was not bare, which eliminates the [Andean] condor. Neither was it a California condor for much the same reasons."

Lyman viewed these and similar accounts matter-of-factly, and in his books and correspondence he expressed annoyance with anyone who suggested that the great birds were a myth. "Be assured," he wrote, "that there were and are a few survivors of a remarkable bird that the Indians and white man called thunderbirds. They inhabit high mountain ranges and are seldom seen."

The supposed rarity of the birds was underscored by Lyman in a letter to the author dated January 12, 1974—the last such communication before his death.

He wrote: "... In the area where they are most often seen, there are people who do not believe they exist. Last summer [1973], Duncan Murphy [a West Coast researcher] came all the way from California to search for one. He was joined by a young man and his wife who was a pilot. They searched the hills from the air. No big bird did they see. Murphy stayed for several days in the Jersey Shore area, interviewing those who have seen these huge birds. No nest has ever been found, and none ever shot."

Lyman believed that the Black Forest thunderbirds were being forced from their home range by civilization. He believed their territory in 1974 was reduced to the southern edge of the Black Forest, "north of the Susquehanna River, between Pine Creek at the east and Kettle Creek at the west. All reports during the past twenty years come from this area," he said. He included in this the numerous 1969–1971 sightings around Jersey Shore, two examples of which follow:

On November 9, 1970, Anna and the late Clyde Mincer watched a huge bird soar over their riverfront home for a period of about fifteen minutes. Later the same day the bird (or another like it) returned, cruising overhead for ten minutes. The estimated wingspan was eighteen feet.

Clyde Mincer described its flight manner (to Robert Lyman, Sr.): "It came over town soaring on the air currents. When it got off it would flap its wings slowly to get back on ... It seemed to have trouble keeping with the currents. It would soar a while, lose altitude and then fly back up."

The following year, on June 8, 1971, a great bird was reported feeding on a dead opossum along Cement Hollow Road, east of Jersey Shore. In a letter to Lyman, one of two witnesses remarked that the bird was "big and filled out. It did not run to take off. It just flapped its wings twice and was up." The estimated wingspan? Again, eighteen feet.

Exaggeration? Myth? Or reality?

Loren Coleman has collected reams of big bird reports from throughout the country. He believes that at least some accounts are accurate and factual. Furthermore, Coleman suggests that the great birds could be a near-relative of the condor—a prehistoric creature known as the teratorn.

Fossil remains of this presumably extinct eight thousand-year-old bird tell of at least three different species: the *Teratornis merriami,* with a wingspan of eleven to twelve feet; the *Teratornis incredibilis,* with a wingspan of nearly seventeen feet, and an Argentine fossil nearly twice the size of the merriami—a bird that stood almost five feet high and had a wingspan of about twenty-four feet.

In his book *Curious Encounters,*[63] Coleman notes that the bones of the teratorns have been found in deposits across the United States, from California to Florida. These deposits are commonly found near sites of human habitation, suggesting a hunter-prey bond.

"Were the Amerindians killing off these birds for their feathers or because the birds had been kidnapping their stock and children?" Coleman asks.

Indeed, there are paleontologists who believe the teratorn was a predator and not a carrion-eater like the condor (although condors, and even turkey vultures, have been known to kill small birds or animals). They support this view by noting that the bird had a long, narrow, hooked beak of a kind that would have enabled it to swallow small animals whole, or rend much larger prey. Perhaps coincidentally, there are Native American stories that suggest the thunderbird was a predator that disemboweled living victims.

Although ornithologists and paleontologists can deduce only so much from fossil remains, most suggest that the teratorn was vulturine—that is, vulture-like or condor-like in appearance. (The huge creature was of the New World family *Cathartidae*, which includes the condors.) Still, considering its size, suspected nature, and appearance, it is evident that the teratorn could have been the thunderbird of legend.

Is it possible that a handful of these birds still exist? Are they even now making their last stand, hiding in the crags and crevices of our country's remaining wilderness? Will we someday find their bones only to realize we discovered them just too late?

NOTES

58. Ivan T. Sanderson, "Thunderbirds Again—and Again," *Pursuit*, April 1972, pp. 40–41.

59. Around 1640, a long struggle ensued between the League of the Iroquois and the powerful Susquehannock Indians for control of the game-rich lands then occupied by the Susquehannocks. The Iroquois at the time consisted of the Senecas, Cayugas, Oneidas, Onondagas, and Mohawks. The struggle became known as the Beaver Wars for the simple reason that beaver pelts were a valued commodity in trading with

the French and English, and the Iroquois had largely depleted their territory of these animals. The fighting continued until about 1676, at which point the Susquehannocks—exhausted by the struggle—were overcome and scattered as a people. An irony here is that many of the Susquehannock refugees were eventually taken in and adopted by the Iroquois.

60. Personal communication from Robert Lyman, Jr., dated November 6, 1974.
61. Robert Lyman, Sr., *Amazing Indeed: Strange Events In The Black Forest, Vol. II,* (Coudersport, PA: the Potter Enterprise, 1973). *Forbidden Land, Vol. I,* appeared 1971.
62. *Amazing Indeed,* p. 95.
63. Loren Coleman, *Curious Encounters*, (Boston: Faber and Faber, Inc., 1985), p. 46.

Chapter Ten:

Giant Wings and Man-Things

On January 7, 1976, Alverico Guajardo and his family were spending a quiet evening in their Brownsville, Texas mobile home when they were disturbed by a noise and vibration from outside. Guajardo, who was in the rear bedroom at the time (about 8:30 P.M.), said something hit the northeast corner of the trailer. He described the noise as being not unlike the sound a "sack of cement" would make if it were shoved against the trailer.

Unable to find a flashlight, the thirty-five-year-old supermarket stock clerk ran to his station wagon parked outside and drove to a vantage point from where the headlights could pinpoint the source of the disturbance. What he saw had him quite literally asking for God's help. Outlined in the headlights was a being "as tall as a man" with huge blazing-red eyes, wings, and "lots of feathers." The creature, he said, had a long beak, and as it stared in his direction a horrible noise issued from its throat.

Terrified, quite literally frozen with fear, Guajardo remained inside the car for about three minutes,

watching as the being backed slowly toward a nearby dirt lane. When Guajardo finally moved, he
rushed to bring neighbors to the scene, only to discover that the creature had disappeared.

Guajardo was not the first person in the Rio
Grande Valley that winter to encounter a mysterious
winged entity, a creature the media quickly dubbed
"Big Bird" with obvious tongue-in-cheek. One of the
first was a San Benito patrol officer, Arturo Padillo.

At about 5:15 A.M., Sunday, December 28, 1975,
Padillo was alone in his patrol car, driving through
the silent town of about fifteen thousand. The new
year was just around the corner, but the Texas
morning was more eerie than festive. "It was misty
and foggy, and I saw something in the air," Padillo
told reporters. The "something" was a creature flying above the street lights, white in color, with a
wingspan of between twelve and fifteen feet.

As the officer watched, the creature passed
over a local *resaca* (a long channel of water cutting
through the community). Padillo noted that it had
a beak nearly a foot long and a long neck that "sort
of bent as it glided." He added that although he had
spent considerable time in the outdoors hunting
wild game and had visited many zoos, this "was
like nothing I ever saw ..." Before he could radio
for another police unit, the strange bird had disappeared from view.

Padillo, however, wasn't the only officer to see
the creature. Homero Galvan watched from a different location and later agreed with Padillo's description, including the wingspan. San Benito Police
Chief Ted Cortez, who publicly backed his men, told
reporters that six weeks earlier a terrified man had
raced into the station insisting that he had spotted a

giant winged creature. According to Cortez, the man declared: "I'm not drunk, I'm sober! But I saw it ..."

Meanwhile, seventy-five miles west of San Benito, Sheriff Ray Alvarez told reporters that for forty-five days rumors had circulated of a giant bird in Starr County, Texas. One story had the bird perched atop the city courthouse. "It's just rumor to me," observed a cautious Alvarez.

On the night after the giant bird appeared over San Benito, residents reported yet another flying object—one without feathers. The object—a disc-like UFO—was seen soaring between the towns of San Benito and Olmito. The sighting was short-lived, however, as the object reportedly vanished by diving into a canal.

Texans weren't alone in reporting UFOs and strange creatures that winter. At the time, a nationwide flap was underway—a surge of strange activity that began early in 1975 and continued into the following year.

In February 1975, the owner of a trailer park a few miles west of Elizabethtown, Pennsylvania, was forced to install floodlights throughout the park after residents repeatedly complained of nocturnal "banging" on the walls of their mobile homes. Police were summoned often, but found no one and nothing to account for the noise. What's more, the noise persisted, although now, under the new lights, residents began seeing a very frightening form.

Elizabeth Cahill, twenty-eight, had returned from a clothing shower at a friend's home when she heard someone rapping at a window. Thinking one of her neighbors was staging a prank, she turned on the outside light and opened the door—only to receive the fright of her life as a gorilla-like "thing" jumped out into the light at the end of the driveway. "At first I thought it was someone dressed up, playing a joke," she said. "But the longer it stood there, staring, without saying anything, the more scared I got."

For a long terrifying moment Cahill faced the creature at the end of the driveway. Then it began advancing toward her. With a scream she retreated inside, fearful the beast would "break down the door. I had this feeling that the longer I stood there, the angrier it got.... There was something about the eyes; they seemed to get shinier. But the mouth never moved."

Cahill immediately telephoned the nearby residence of Maurice Hiller and family. The Hillers arrived with air rifles (the only available weapons) and the family Irish setter. When they searched the grounds, they found nothing. According to Cahill: "It had snowed that night, yet there were no tracks. Even if it was someone dressed up in a costume, he would have left tracks."

Describing the creature, she said it was the height of an "average-sized man," covered with "smooth-looking" fur, and had an "apish face, yet not exactly [like that of an ape]," and stood with "bent legs and arms."

Soon others in the park were reporting "manimal" encounters. One woman said a gorilla-like creature came at her and grabbed at her coat. She managed to evade it only because she left her coat in its arms. Another individual, a man of about forty, was entering the trailer court one night around 8:00 P.M. when his auto headlights caught and illuminated a "big gorilla" ambling casually through the park.

In August 1975, a small group of boys (ages twelve to fifteen) were playing ball on the grounds of the nearby Londonderry Elementary School when—once again—a manimal was spotted, this time wandering toward the school from an adjoining field. None of the players remained long enough to see if the creature wanted to join their game.

Throughout 1975, weird events continued around the park, reaching a peak in August before tapering off. Then, in February and March 1976 there came a renewal of the mysterious knocking on trailer walls and more reports of strange creatures moving on the grounds at night.

On March 29, 1976, Mr. and Mrs. Roger Williams (a pseudonym) were retiring for the night when Mrs. Williams saw "a bright light" illuminate the grounds that separated the trailer park from several acres of adjacent pine woods. The time was about 11:30 P.M. Just as she was about to dismiss the flash as being of no importance, a strange "growling" began just outside the bedroom window. Alarmed, she roused her husband, who had neither observed the light flash nor heard the growl. "He told me to forget it, that it was my stomach growling," Mrs. Williams said. "Then we both heard it."

Grabbing his shotgun, Roger Williams stormed out the door and around to the rear of the mobile home. Later, his wife said he mentioned seeing a "dark upright shape" ambling toward the pine woods. However, Williams was less certain when I spoke with him. "I didn't see anything," he repeatedly said. When his wife persisted about the dark shape, he continued a posture of denial: "No, I saw nothing. There are no such things as monsters—or flying saucers. After all, this is 1976 ... that growling could have been a big dog." Williams, however, was unable to explain an earlier episode involving his young daughter.

During an afternoon in August 1975, the child was playing inside the mobile home when she happened to glance out the living room window into the back yard. She later told her parents that she saw a "big bear" attempting to hide behind a tree. The time was around 3:00 P.M. The child was so frightened by the creature that she lay prone on the floor until her parents returned home some minutes later.

When asked about the "bear," the girl said it was tall, perhaps taller than her father (about five feet, eight inches), and had "reddish brown" hair. The hair itself was moderately long. During a visit to the Williams home, I asked the daughter if she could recognize the creature as anything she may have seen on television, or in a zoo. She replied that the beast actually looked more like a large "monkey" than a bear. To the relief of the child, she had not seen it since.

In an attempt to independently verify the trailer park sightings, I spoke with a representative of the Pennsylvania State Police and was told that frightened park residents had indeed reported encounters with "hairy beasts." Troopers were sent often to investigate, but police were not the only men in uniform to visit the park.

According to various residents, the Army National Guard arrived in August 1976 in jeeps and military trucks and posted a watch at both entrances to the grounds. When approached by residents, the soldiers would reply only that they were there for "official reasons."

On January 2, 1976, creature tracks were found on the outskirts of Harlington, Texas. According to news accounts, the prints—large and three-toed—were discovered behind the home of Mr. Stanley Lawson.

The tracks were about twelve inches long and six to eight inches wide. They marked a trail eighty yards long across an open field before abruptly ending. Jackie Davies, fourteen, and Tracey Lawson, eleven, cousins who were playing in the Lawson backyard, later told Ray Norton, news director of KGBT-TV in Harlington, that the tracks were made on January 1 by a huge black bird with red eyes, a sharp beak, and a "gorilla like" face. They said they had spotted the creature in the field and had taken a closer look with binoculars from the house. The girls watched until the creature disappeared from view. When it suddenly reappeared nearer to their location, they fled into the house. Norton filmed the tracks for broadcast on his station.

Tracks of a similar nature have appeared in various locations throughout the country. On September 21, 1973, three-toed prints were discovered in Westmoreland County, Pennsylvania. The tracks were found after two terrified boys ran into the state police barracks in Greensburg and told troopers they had observed "the head and shoulders of a gorilla-like creature" in a section of woods near the edge of the community. When troopers and civilian investigators went to the site, they found three-toed footprints "deeply impressed" in the soft earth, measuring about fourteen by seven and one-half inches.[64] Three-toed tracks were also found in northwestern New Jersey in August 1976, near the rural residential area of White Meadow Lake. Encounters with hairy man-beasts and UFOs were numerous at the time, as were reports of animal mutilations.

On January 12, 1976, the Harlington Police Department received a report of a large bird just off Interstate 83. When officers investigated, they found a "decoy" made from palm leaves and sticks. Two days later Arturo Rodriguez, nineteen, and his nine-year-old nephew, Ricardo, saw something a little more lively, and a little more frightening.

At sundown, the two were fishing along the bank of the Rio Grande River, as they often did. According to Rodriguez, there was a rustling overhead and when they looked up, they both saw a great, gray bird gliding at a height of about fifty feet. As with the San Benito sightings, the bird apparently did not flap its wings. Rodriguez told authorities that on seeing the creature they simply ran "like the devil was after us." The bird, he remarked, had a wingspan of fifteen to twenty feet and a body the size of "a small man."

Two hours later, Roberto Gonzalez, twenty-four, was driving parallel to the Rio Grande River along Interstate 83 in the direction of Laredo. Approaching an area of oil fields, he observed what appeared to be a giant bird silhouetted against the clouds, some sixty feet in the air.

Around mid-January 1976, Libby and Deany Ford of Brownsville, Texas were driving home after school when they spotted a "big black bird." The girls, who were interviewed by reporters from KGBT-TV, said the creature was as large as a small man and had a "face like a bat." After looking through an anthropology book, they decided the thing looked a lot like a prehistoric pteronodon—a flying dinosaur.

As the sightings accumulated, authorities—searching for a prosaic explanation—speculated that the winged creature was an escaped zoo bird, or a wild condor, or maybe even a great blue heron. The director of the Gladys Porter Zoo in Brownsville, who had been queried repeatedly about the creature, denied that the zoo had any escaped birds. He also said he doubted the bird was a California or Andean condor, as neither species was ever found in South Texas. As for the great blue heron: in flight, with long neck tucked in and legs extended straight back, this bird does appear prehistoric and reptilian. In late July 1989, my sister, Donna M. Boltz, and her son, Jeremy, watched what was almost certainly a great blue as it soared above their car. Silhouetted against a moonlit sky, their immediate reaction was that the bird looked an awful lot like a pterodactyl. Later, after careful rethinking, it became apparent that the bird was indeed a heron.

It's doubtful that a heron was responsible for the many giant bird sightings in and around the Rio Grande Valley in late 1975 and early 1976. With a seventy-inch wingspan and a length of about thirty-eight inches, the great blue hardly matches the reported size of the creature witnessed by Alverico Guajardo, or by officers Padillo and Galvan. Most likely we'll never know what was aloft that winter in South Texas.

Strange winged entities, while not reported as often as UFOs or even as frequently as manimals and phantom panthers, are nonetheless witnessed too often to be easily dismissed. On September 12, 1880, the *New York Times* reported the appearance of something that looked like "a man with bat's wings and improved frog's legs" flying over Coney Island. The entity was seen by "many reputable persons," the *Times* reported.

On January 6, 1948, United States Army officials at McChord Field, Chehalis, Washington, were informed of the appearance of a flying man over the area. Witnesses said the man was equipped with a pair of silver wings, fastened by some type of a strap. The Army, not surprisingly, did not investigate.

Our friend the man-bat turned up again in June 1953 in Houston, Texas. According to various news accounts, several persons outside an East Third Street apartment observed what appeared to be a bat-winged, man-sized figure dressed in dark, tight-fitting clothes. The sighting occurred at about 2:30 A.M. The man-bat leaped into a pecan tree and remained there for a time before disappearing. A moment later there was a white flash, after which "a torpedo-shaped thing" flew over the housetops across the street.

In 1967, in the Point Pleasant, West Virginia, area, fearful residents were stalked by a man-sized winged creature with glowing red eyes. The media labeled the thing "Mothman." The appearance of the creature coincided with persistent UFO activity and reports of bizarre animal mutilations. John Keel later documented these and other occurrences in his now classic *The Mothman Prophecies*.[65]

Over the years, mainstream science has dealt with reports of mysterious creatures in the same way it has handled stories about UFOs. The reports are either ignored or dismissed with contempt.

In 1856, zoologists contemptuously dismissed the report of an explorer who claimed to have encountered a huge, hairy man-beast in the African Congo. The creature stood "nearly six feet high, with immense body, huge chest, and great muscular arms ..." The explorer was Paul du Chaillu, and he was the first white man to encounter the gorilla.

Eighty years later, in 1936, the elusive giant panda of Tibet (western China) was found and transported to the United States for exhibit in Chicago's

Brookfield Zoo.⁶⁶ The black and white bear-like animal (actually related to the raccoon) was for many years thought to be only a myth. Like the gorilla before it, such an animal could not and did not exist, zoologists claimed. It wasn't until the 1936 expedition—organized by animal collector and adventurer William H. Harkness—that the naysayers were finally silenced.

More recently, expeditions organized by the World Wildlife Fund turned up the remains (three sets of horns and the upper skulls) of a new species of Asian mammal, and then the mammal itself. Local hunting trophies revealed the creature to be bovid, and it is now known as the Vu Quang ox. The discovery was made in the lush Vu Quang Nature Reserve, a forest region along the Laotian–Vietnamese border. Evidence was also found—during the initial expedition in 1992—of two previously unknown bird species, a new fish, and an unknown variety of tortoise.

Most wildlife discoveries are made accidentally by hard-working amateurs, or by poorly funded field zoologists. Deskbound bureaucrats masquerading as scientists, meanwhile, are forever proclaiming that there is nothing new or different under the sun. Unfortunately, in our post-industrial, satellite-linked world—a world where our remaining wilderness areas are fast dwindling— unknown animal species are probably dying off far faster than we can identify them. The next animal registered in the zoological record books could be an endangered Bigfoot (sasquatch). Or the melanistic puma of eastern North America. Or perhaps the giant condor-like bird of the East and Midwest. These creatures, like the gorilla and the giant panda of an earlier era, cannot and do not exist, according to science.

There are, however, other mysterious creatures at large in the land: beasts that, to quote Loren Coleman, seem to move in a "smoke screen" of more acceptable sightings. These creatures look like pumas but leave tracks showing non-retractable claws. They look like hairy man-beasts but have only three toes instead of five, and have glowing red eyes. They look like huge birds but on close approach are often more man-like than bird-like; and they all appear and disappear at will and seem to have no place in an orderly, modern world.

Years ago, I adopted the expression "para-creature" to categorize such beasts. In past ages they were probably responsible for stories of men transformed into monsters, so perhaps "were-beast" is a better term. By whatever name, they have stalked the fields and forests of our planet for hundreds or thousands of years. They sow fear and confusion, and cause havoc wherever they appear. In many cases, they appear in areas frequented by UFOs or odd nocturnal lights, leading some investigators to suspect a connection. Other researchers have gone so far as to suggest that all of these creatures, along with UFOs and similar oddities, are part of a singular global or even cosmic process that we, as humans, barely recognize, let alone understand.

Whatever the source, whatever the cause, one thing is certain: the manimals, the winged weirdos, the phantom panthers will all continue to appear ... treading soundly on our beliefs and changing our dreams into nightmares.

NOTES

64. Allen V. Noe, "ABSMal Affairs In Pennsylvania and Elsewhere," *Pursuit*, October 1973, pp. 84–89. Sightings of man-beasts were frequent in Westmoreland County, Pennsylvania, during the summer of 1973. Noe, and other members of the Society for the Investigation of the Unexplained, visited the area and worked closely with Stan Gordon, then director of the Pennsylvania Association for Study of the Unexplained. Three-toed tracks, as well as hair and fecal specimens of an unknown animal, were found throughout the area during the summer. Most witnesses reported large ape-like creatures accompanied by a smell like sulfur or rotten eggs or "rotten meat." They also reported eyes that glowed "orange-red" in the dark.

65. John A. Keel, *The Mothman Prophecies* (Avondale Estates, Georgia: Illuminet Press, 1991). Originally published in New York by Saturday Review Press (1975).

66. Loren Coleman, *Tom Slick and The Search for the Yeti* (Boston: Faber and Faber, Inc., 1989), p. 19.

Chapter Eleven:

"Until you've been there ..."

In October 1987, researchers spent two days scanning the depths of Loch Ness in northern Scotland with state-of-the-art sonar. The intent was to study fish distribution and map the lake bottom, and, if possible, find evidence supporting the existence of the lake's fabled monster. The operation was called "Deepscan," and it was the brainchild of Adrian Shine, a longtime Loch Ness researcher and an expert on fishery habitat. Lowrance Electronics of Tulsa, Oklahoma provided the technical expertise and hardware.

Because of the nature of the study, a good deal of hype surrounded Deepscan. Newspapers and television provided voluminous coverage, much of it slightly tongue-in-cheek. Spectators crowded the nearby town of Drumnadrochit and along the loch shores. The atmosphere was circus-like but not the aim: more than twenty boats and their crews and technicians were involved in probing the extremely deep, cold lake.

Deepscan was, in fact, the next step in Adrian Shine's continuing study of Loch Ness. The researcher is credited with being first to probe the loch with sport fishing sonar[67]—an effort that yielded some rather startling findings and prompted him to approach Lowrance about a more extensive survey.

According to Steve Schneider, a spokesman for Lowrance, "It was only after Shine began using sonar, back in the mid–'70s, that anyone was aware of really large schools of fish in Loch Ness." Elaborating, Schneider noted that some of the fish were eventually caught and identified as Arctic char (*Salvelinus alpinus*)—a variety of small-scaled trout common to cold northern waters. The discovery was a huge surprise, even to the Scots who have lived for generations along the loch shores.

"Until you've been there, it's just incomprehensible to anyone from the States how little is known about that body of water," declared Schneider. "Those people have lived along that shore for hundreds of years, and have no idea of what's in there." Demonstrating his point, Schneider noted that local anglers traditionally take to the water with fly rods in fourteen-foot wooden rowboats. Their quarry are the Atlantic salmon, which, along with char and brown trout, appear to make up the bulk of the loch's fishery. "If the fish aren't within six feet of the surface," he said, "they don't catch them."

Another reason so little is known about Loch Ness, Schneider observed, is that the British scientific community avoids the lake. Any research there would imply an active investigation of the monster—which, after all, is not supposed to exist. Fortunately not all scientists, or talented lay researchers, are susceptible to such dogma.

In conceiving Operation Deepscan, Shine and his supporters outlined four purely scientific objectives:

1. Gain information about an unidentified species of fish on the lake bottom, in more than seven hundred feet of water. (This is deeper by far than the Arctic char, which hold at about two hundred feet by day and ascend to within fifty feet of the surface by night.)
2. Graph, for the first time, the loch's deepest waters.
3. Compile charts for a "map" showing fish distribution in the loch, and obtain data on unusual thermal patterns for later study.
4. Locate and mark objects of interest on the lake bottom for later examination with underwater television equipment.

These objectives were, of course, wrapped around the well publicized search for "Nessie"—or rather, for evidence of a breeding colony of creatures, since sightings of a huge animal in the loch date back to about A.D. 565.

Legend has it that fourteen centuries ago, an Irish saint named Columba confronted a huge creature shortly after it devoured a hapless Pict near a ferry crossing. Warned about the monster by mourners of the dead man, Columba stated his wish to cross over regardless. Since the ferry was on the far side of the loch, he directed a follower to swim over and return with the boat. As the swimmer entered deep water, he was approached by a huge beast that seemed determined to make a snack of him. But the saint would have none of it. He raised his hand and invoked the name of God. His actions, we are told, forced the beast into retreat, after which it vanished back into the depths.

Though probably more myth than fact, Columba's encounter is the earliest documented story about a creature in the loch. Later accounts show up rarely over the next several centuries. Then in the early 1700s, the construction of new roads brought more travelers into the formerly isolated highlands, and reports of a creature became much more frequent.

The first real road along the loch was built on the north shore by British soldiers, many of whom reported seeing "whales." It was assumed, at the time, that whales might have entered from the North Sea through large underwater passages. While this remains doubtful, it is possible, indeed even probable, that in much earlier times when the loch was open to the sea, whales, along with other forms of sea life, moved back and forth quite freely.

A narrow steep-sided body, Loch Ness was formed by long-ago glacial action. It stretches some twenty-four miles and is part of a gorge known as the Great Glen, which runs from the city of Inverness on the east to Loch Linnhe on the west. The Great Glen was formed millions of years ago and was connected to the North Sea. As glaciers came and went, the Glen was cut even deeper. Finally, the retreating ice closed the mouth of the gorge, filling it with massive amounts of sediment, soil, and rocks, leaving behind Loch Ness.

Averaging seven hundred feet overall and dropping to a maximum of 975 feet, Loch Ness is the largest freshwater lake in volume in Great Britain and the third largest in Europe. Its waters are brooding and dark—heavily saturated with microscopic particles of peat which run off from the surrounding hillsides into tributary rivers and streams. The heavy peat concentration limits underwater visibility to a few feet, creating a special problem for those who would try to photograph the loch depths—or any monster that it might contain.

But in 1972, and again in 1975, underwater photos were in fact taken of a large animal in the loch. The photos were the result of expeditions conducted by members of the Academy of Applied Science in Belmont, Massachusetts. During an earlier expedition in 1970, Academy members recorded images on a sonar graph after something quite large passed in front of a high-frequency sonar unit in Urquhart Bay. Cameras were not used that year. Sonar was used again in 1972, but a camera-strobe system was added, permitting underwater photos at distances of up to ten feet. One of the photos (computer-enhanced for clarity) showed a close-up of what looked like a paddle-shaped flipper. In 1975, other images were captured on high-speed film. The head, neck, and upper torso of a "creature" estimated to be about eighteen feet long appeared in one photo. Another showed a close-up of what may have been the creature's head.

In a published account summarizing the expeditions, researchers Robert H. Rines, Charles W. Wyckoff, Harold E. Edgerton, and Martin Klein reported that at about 1:00 A.M. on August 8, 1972, the night the flipper photo was taken: "... salmon were seen jumping away from something in the loch, and this flight was also seen on sonar. At the same time, a large object came back into the beam, and a bit later a second object of similar size. These objects were separated by about twelve feet; they were, indeed, distinct objects. During this period, photographs were obtained of what was in the beam."[68]

For a time, the Academy photos stirred up considerable excitement—enough, at any rate, so that a scientific name was assigned to the creature: *Nessiteras rhombopteryx* ("the Ness marvel with the

diamond-shaped fin"). By granting the creature scientific status, British lawmakers were able to protect
Nessie under the National Conservation of Wildlife
Act. Unfortunately, a more ambitious expedition in
1976 failed to turn up anything new, and in many
circles interest faded and skepticism was reborn.
Today few outside the scientific community (and
probably very few within) even recall that the animal
was ever granted protection.

As impressive as the Academy photos were and are,
the bulk of evidence of something unusual in the
loch has come from the many photos, films, and
videos of Nessie taken by tourists and amateur
enthusiasts. Some of the photos are obvious hoaxes
while others have been subjected to intense scrutiny
by experts who could find no flaw or evidence of
tampering. Add this to the Academy photos and
sonar tracings, and a point in favor of Nessie could
be proven in any court of law.

Yet, despite all the sightings, despite the visual
evidence of photos, film, video, and sonar, the scientific community, for the most part, remains hesi-
tant to take a close look at the mystery of Loch
Ness. Even the Academy expeditions, although well-
planned and executed, were the work of technolo-
gists (and not zoologists) operating with limited
funds. Other research carried out at the loch has
been on an even smaller scale—the work of individuals paying their own way.

Not so with Operation Deepscan. Recognizing the
tremendous public relations potential in a massive
sonar sweep of the loch, Lowrance Electronics, a man-
ufacturer of sport fishing sonar, came up with a reported $1.6 million in combined funds, equipment, and

support for naturalist Adrian Shine, who organized the search and served as field leader. Several sponsors were involved, among them Continental Airlines, which provided flight certificates for the Lowrance staff and for forty journalists from the United States. In dollars alone the project dwarfed the disappointing 1976 Academy expedition, funded by the *New York Times* for a reported seventy-five thousand dollars.

To accomplish the objectives of Deepscan, Shine and his backers equipped more than twenty power boats and several high-speed chase boats with state-of-the-art Lowrance X–16 sonar systems. The power boats, running abreast, swept the length of the lake. Two sweeps were made, one on each day of the operation—October 9 and 10, 1987.

More than three hundred press and media representatives from twenty-two nations were on hand for the search. Headquarters was in Drumnadrochit, site of the Loch Ness Exhibition Centre (founded in 1980). Excitement escalated quickly as reports filtered in of sonar contact.

Three times that first day contact was made with large, moving objects: one at 192 feet, another at 176 feet. The third target was much deeper—606 feet (185 meters), charted for about two minutes. Curiously, the deep contact was made by a chase boat, and not one of the power boats.

Though equipped with identical X–16 sonar units, the chase boats were expected to do no more than verify contact made by the slow-moving line of cruisers. In this instance, the only detection was by chase crew. By the time other boats moved in, the target had vanished.

According to Schneider, all three contacts were in the vicinity of Urquhart Castle, overlooking Urquhart

Bay. Here, beyond the bay, the loch drops to its maximum depth of 975 feet. Here too, more sightings have been made than at any other point along the loch.

But a question arises: How did the deep contact, the object at 606 feet, manage to avoid the main sonar net only to be detected by a chase boat? Actually, said Schneider, there are four plausible explanations.

The first explanation requires a bit of explaining itself. Sonar waves are cone-shaped pulses of sound—narrow at the point of broadcast but widening as they move away. During Deepscan, the downward focused beams from each cruiser came close or overlapped in deep water to form what was essentially a single field.[69] However, closer to the surface there were gaps great enough to admit the proverbial tractor-trailer rig—or in this case, a large aquatic animal, which then descended to six hundred feet.

Another explanation, one favored by Schneider, is that the target was resting motionless on the bottom, perhaps along a drop-off or in a rocky crevice, and simply did not register on sonar. (Even allowing for recent improvements, sonar is still an imprecise tool.) The target then ascended, and was spotted by the chase boat.

A third explanation is that the target slipped around either end of the line of power boats, since the line did not entirely cover the one-mile width of the loch.

Finally, there is a real possibility that the target was not in the main loch body when the line of boats moved by. According to Schneider, Urquhart Bay was never sonar scanned, since the water there is generally less than one hundred feet deep. In view of this, he admitted it is possible that something large moved out of the bay after the power boats passed by.

Despite the first day's success, no additional contacts were made on the second and final day. Still, Operation Deepscan could hardly be considered a failure. It had met most of its purely scientific objectives (information on the unidentified fish species was still forthcoming), and had provided additional "hard" evidence (the paper graph tracings) that something quite large exists in the loch.

Unfortunately, images on a sonar graph mean little to skeptical and impatient members of the press and media. As Shine himself observed before a crowd of reporters, "You want me to hand you the Loch Ness Monster." Since he obviously could not do this, most members of the media viewed Deepscan as just another failed monster hunt.

But the sonar tracings were, and are, significant. Moreover, the confirmation that much of the loch is an untapped fishery instead of being a relatively lifeless lake sheds a new light on reports of large aquatic animals.

Consider this: those who disbelieve in the animal have long argued that the loch's food base is much too small. Big beasts have big appetites, after all, and there was no reason to suspect large schools of fish moving deep in the loch. True, the Scots and English knew about the salmon and brown trout, but based on their catch experience they no doubt underestimated the numbers of those fish. Anglers from the United States and Canada, long used to working with sonar and deep trolling equipment, could have explained it to them: never judge a lake by its surface. This accounts for the great surprise when

Shine, using downrigger gear[70], caught the first Arctic char, and the even bigger surprise when Deepscan verified large numbers of these and other fish.

Which leaves us with speculation about the kind of animal apparently dining on the loch's fish. While opinions vary, the most popular answer is found in the town of Drumnadrochit, where a life-size model of a plesiosaur—an aquatic dinosaur—has been erected for tourist consumption.

Of course, the plesiosaur[71] is thought to have died out some sixty million years ago (though there are vast gaps in our fossil records of such creatures). Also, critics suggest that the plesiosaur could not have survived the period of glacial activity during which the loch was formed. Those who say this ignore the revisionist theory that most (if not all) of the saurians were warm-blooded, and not cold, and therefore adaptable to environmental change, just as mammals are adaptable.

Still other persons, including Adrian Shine, have suggested that the creature is a giant sturgeon—a family of prehistoric fish related to the paddlefish which can grow to in excess of twenty feet and weigh up to a ton. The sturgeon (of which there are both fresh and saltwater species) is a bottom-feeder, living mainly on crustaceans and other invertebrates. It doesn't feed on large fish and is seldom found near the surface. It does, during early spring, move into tributary streams and rivers to spawn. If there are giant sturgeon in Loch Ness, say in excess of four hundred pounds, they should be present in the River Ness and tributary waters during the spawn, and yet they are not reported. I've fished cold-water lakes in Quebec, nearly as deep as Loch Ness and every bit as dark. Here can be found one of the largest species of North American freshwater fish, the lake, or red, sturgeon. This fish is almost never seen except during the spawn, when it is routinely netted by Cree Indians.

In some areas of the world, the sturgeon has been fished almost to extinction. Meanwhile, other forms of primitive marine life keep turning up. One well known example was the coelacanth (pronounced *see-la-canth*), an ancient lobe-finned fish some five feet in length and dating back four hundred million years—actually predating the dinosaurs. The first known specimen was discovered on December 22, 1938, amid the catch of a South African fishing boat, by the naturalist Marjorie Courtenay-Latimer. At the time of discovery, the species had been thought extinct for at least eighty million years. A second was discovered fourteen years later, on December 24, 1952, in the Comoro Islands. Others have since been found, and in 1987, a West German team in the submersible Geo filmed six of the creatures at a depth of several hundred feet.[72] Unfortunately, coelacanths seem to be few in number and the species may now be on the brink of true extinction.

Yet another example of primitive fish is the "megamouth"—a species of plankton-eating shark, hitherto unknown, accidentally caught by the Navy some years ago in waters near Hawaii. Since then, other megamouths have turned up, including a sixteen-foot specimen captured alive, radio-tagged, released, and tracked for two days in late October 1990.[73] In view of all this, who is to say whether the plesiosaur really is extinct?

Meanwhile, at Loch Ness the curious gather each summer with cameras and binoculars. They walk the overlooks and strain their eyes—hoping for a glimpse of a monster.

NOTES
67. Though Shine was first with sport fishing sonar, others were ahead of him with high-frequency, side-scan sonar. This type of instrument is often towed behind a vessel and used in such applications as mapping the ocean bottom during offshore oil exploration.

68. Robert H. Rines, Charles W. Wyckoff, Harold E. Edgerton, and Martin Klein, *Technology Review*, March/April 1976, published by the Alumni Association of the Massachusetts Institute of Technology [reprinted in *Pursuit*, Summer 1976, pp. 56–58].

69. At the time of Operation Deepscan, a Lowrance Electronics spokesman noted that when sonar units are operated in proximity, with transmitted patterns overlapping, electronic interference from one unit to another is commonplace since they all "speak the same frequency." The X–16 unit used during the expedition is different, however, in that its sonar has a discrimination feature that recognizes only the returning signal sent by that particular unit. Thus, multiple units can be used without frequency interference.

70. Downrigger gear enables an angler to deep-troll a lure or a live bait at exact depths. Experienced deep-water anglers use downriggers in conjunction with sonar, and can fish as deep as the lines on their reels allow.

71. A two-ton corpse resembling a plesiosaur was hauled aboard the *Zuyvo Maru*, a Japanese

trawler off Christchurch, New Zealand on April 25, 1977. Netted at a depth of nine hundred feet, the dead beast measured thirty-two feet and had a long neck, long tail, four fins or flippers, and a well-developed spine. The carcass was seen by eighteen crewmen and at least one passenger— Michihiko Yano, an assistant production manager of Taiyo Fisheries, Ltd., who measured the rotting mass and took tissue samples and color photos for return to Japan before it was tossed overboard.

72. "The Coelacanth—50 Years Later," *The ISC Newsletter*, Spring 1989.
73. "Megamouth VI Caught Alive and Studied," *The ISC Newsletter*, Summer 1991, published by the International Society of Cryptozoology, edited by J. Richard Greenwell.

Chapter Twelve:

"Something plodding heavily through the forest"

I n the waning years of the nineteenth century, stories began emerging from the Himalayas about a species of shy, hairy hominid occasionally glimpsed in the high mountain recesses. The animal, known to the natives of Tibet, Nepal, Bhutan, and Sikkim as *metoh kangami* ("abominable or filthy man of the snow"), or *yeti* (from the Sherpa *yeh-teh* or *mi-te*—roughly translated as "man-bear"), became known to westerners as the "abominable snowman" because of a misspelling of the former name and a resulting false translation.

By the mid to late 1950s, yeti stories were fairly commonplace in the press, with attention focused on a handful of early cryptozoologists who were singularly intent on capturing one of the creatures.[74] Meanwhile, reports of a yeti-like animal began to issue from Canada and the Northwestern United States, where the creature was known to Native Americans as sasquatch, or to the Anglo population as "Bigfoot" because of the large tracks sometimes found in dense forest regions.

I was still a young boy, perhaps seven or eight, when I first became aware of the stories about yeti and sasquatch. I was electrified. Suddenly the world was vast and filled with mystery; if yeti were possible, then anything was possible. With a little help from my mother I was able to follow the newspaper accounts about the early Himalayan expeditions. Sometimes the subject came up at the dinner table. My father always expressed doubt about the yeti's existence, while my mother took the opposite view. And yet, there were times when I was certain my mother was the real skeptic and my father the one who harbored a willingness to believe. No matter. The dinner table discussions always lit my imagination. They caused a thrill of excitement, and even a little fear.

Many years later, when reports of Bigfoot began surfacing in the eastern United States, I sought out and interviewed some of the presumed witnesses. In some cases the percipient described a beast which, for many reasons, seemed more supernatural than natural. In other cases, the information proved to be second or third hand ... a story about someone who knew someone else who saw "something."

Then I met Roy W. "Indiana" Jones. Roy's story was quite unlike most of the sasquatch tales I had previously heard. A first-person account, it was richly detailed with many small, verifiable points, and I soon found I had little reason to doubt its authenticity. At the time of the telling, Roy was an active-duty Air Force recruiter in York, Pennsylvania. His account, summarized one day during lunch, grabbed my full attention. I wanted to hear more and when I suggested recording the story for later publication, he agreed.

Roy's experience had occurred twenty years earlier on a plot of land called Prince of Wales Island. To be sure, there are two islands by this name. One is a large landmass found in the Arctic Circle; the other is considerably smaller (though not exactly tiny), located just off the west coast of Alaska. This second, smaller island was Roy's destination in 1969, when he accompanied his father, the late Richard L. Jones, and a friend, Roy "Buster" Lee, on expedition.

At the time of the expedition, Richard Jones was in the gemstone business—locating, mining, and selling semi-precious stones and crystals. In earlier days he had flirted briefly with treasure hunting. When this proved unprofitable he switched to stones, as there was a ready market among private collectors.

Jones had been aware of a previous expedition to Prince of Wales—an operation staffed and financed by the Smithsonian Institution. That expedition had been after a rare type of gemstone—a green crystal that would fetch handsomely among collectors, Jones decided. Through an acquaintance at the Smithsonian, the well-known mineralogist and author Paul Desautels (*The Mineral Kingdom*, 1968), he was able to obtain sufficient information to plan his own trip to the remote location.

At this point begins the narrative of his son Roy Jones:

> Prince of Wales is a pretty good sized place, about twenty-five miles long and ten or twelve miles wide. It is heavily forested ... a rain forest with a couple of hundred inches per year of precipitation. To my knowledge, there are two settlements on the far western side. One is a little place called Hyder, and I can't recall the name of the other. Hyder is a fishing village ... just a few people. There are no roads anywhere on the island because there are no [other] settlements.

The [United States] Forest Service has a few scattered cabins, which may be rented.

The reason we picked this particular place [Prince of Wales] is because of a mineral deposit called *epidote*, which is an iron/copper/aluminum silicate which forms really large, dark green crystals—kind of an olive green. This is probably the second most famous locale in the world for epidote, the other being a place called Knappenwand, which is in Austria, and which produces crystals that have a more gem-like quality and are a little more delicate.

Prince of Wales Island is an area of the world where, with different kinds of geology, you have what is called 'contact geology' ... dissimilar rock types, such as hot volcanic, or magnetic, coming in contact with sedimentary kinds of things, and a hot junction [established] between the two. A lot of different elements combine and recombine and form crystals and such along the contact zone. But because [the island] literally is an out-of-the-way place, not many people make an effort to get in there—you practically have to mount an expedition, which of course is what we did. So we saved our bucks and hired a bush pilot to fly us to a lake on the island.

There were three of us on the trip, my dad, myself, and Roy Lee. I've lost contact with Roy over the years—he lives in Southwest Arizona or California somewhere. Roy is about my age [forty-five in 1995]. I went to high school with him. We called him 'Buster.' He was a big kid, about 6'2" or 6'3", around two hundred pounds—not one to be intimidated by much of anything.

We mounted our expedition into Prince of Wales from Ketchikan [Alaska]. The lake we landed on is called Lake Josephine, which was on the topographic maps, and is a good-sized lake nestled between three mountains. We had to spiral down into it to make the landing. Taking off was a real project, too. As soon as you lifted off, you immediately had to start turning and banking—you had to spiral out of this place to get over the surrounding peaks. Sort of like being in the bottom of a teacup.

The island is heavily forested—enormous pine trees and lots of vegetation and, as I'd said, an incredible amount of rainfall. We landed all of our supplies on the shore—we had rented one of those little cabins, and that's the reason we picked Lake Josephine as a base of operations, because there was an available forest service cabin. We felt we might need some solid shelter instead of living out of tents. But it didn't put us exactly where we needed to be—we needed to be [at a place] about three or four miles [from the camp], where in the 1920s and 1930s a geology team had gone looking for copper deposits. They were the folks who discovered the epidote crystals. A later expedition [the Smithsonian team, in 1965] went in to bring out crystals, but their trip was done specifically to provide materials for the Smithsonian. We were doing it for profit. A small cluster of crystals about thumb size, two or three of them stuck together, even at that time—would bring $250 to $275. So it was going to be a very profitable trip.

We arrived on the island in the middle of June, about the 14th or 15th of June. It was still too early. There was snow on the ground, ice on the lake when we landed. We had to bust through the ice to get the aircraft to shore—bust through about seventy yards of ice, hanging onto the pontoons. If you can imagine this: the engine is revving so we can bring the pontoons of the aircraft onto the shelf of ice. I'm hanging off the tip of a pontoon, banging on the ice with a sledgehammer, crushing the ice. We had to back the airplane out the same way, to a place where we had broken up enough ice so it could be turned around [for departure].[75]

There was quite a bit of snow around the cabin, which had a Dutch door. Inside the cabin was a little oil burner stove and a couple of bunk areas and a table. It wasn't very big, nothing more than four walls, maybe ten by twelve feet.

This time of year it was daylight for a long period of time—it was only dark from about 10:30 P.M. to 2:00 A.M., so the snow melted quickly during the next couple of days. It took us a couple of days to set up [camp]. We were located between two lakes, one of them Lake Josephine. There was a narrow isthmus between the two lakes. The mountain we had to reach was called, of all things, Green Monster Mountain.

I suspect the name 'Green Monster' came from the original [copper] expedition members, who may have talked about the 'monstrous' green crystals located there. No proof of this—just supposition on my part. At any rate, the mountain is 'L' shaped; one leg of it runs north and south and the other runs east and west. The elevation change was probably about two thousand feet, from the level we were at, at the lake, to where we needed to go to the collecting site. We needed to go about four to five miles to get to this area.

First to try and locate the mine site were Buster Lee and Richard Jones. But according to Roy, the two were unsuccessful. A second attempt was made the following day, this time by Roy and Buster.

Trying to find a path, we started in one direction around this lake—not Josephine but the other lake—and we almost lost it the first time we tried to go in that direction.

There was an incredible gorge that emptied water out of the second lake ... about a seven hundred- or eight hundred-foot drop. The water emptied and fell and went on out to the ocean only a couple of miles away. We were coming around the edge of the lake and thinking this was no big deal, that we could somehow get through there, and we came to this jumble of logs blocking the gorge. The gorge was only about fifteen or twenty feet across at this point, but seven hundred or eight hundred feet down. It took your breath away: when you looked down, it basically scared the hell out of you. I don't like working at height like that; but the man with me, Buster, was busy trying to figure out how to cross this area, this jumble of logs, and these were good-sized logs … about three or four feet in diameter.

There was one log about a foot and a half to two feet under the water's surface, and Buster said, 'Well, I can get on this thing and walk across to the other side.' I said, 'Oh my God, this isn't very solid, I'm not too sure about this!' Anyway, Buster stepped out onto the log, and was not quite up to his knees in cold, icy water. He stepped out with one foot, then the other— and he had nothing to hold onto. Then the log buoyed down, and Buster went into the water about up to his armpits! I was sure he was gone. I mean, the water was moving pretty swiftly and here he was in this [current] up to his armpits, and I don't know how he ever stayed on the log. I was scared out of my wits, because there was nothing I could do to prevent him from going over; and then the log buoyed back up and he was again in water up to his knees.[76]

I said to him, 'Well, what now, Ace?' And he said, 'I'm going on across.' He said, 'If I have to, I can practically jump from here.' He took it real easy and slow and made it across. I told him he was out of his mind if he thought I was going to cross. But he said, 'No, no, come on, it's fine!' Somehow he managed to entice me across this log.

One thing we noticed was that this particular location had to be a major crossing for practically every critter in the countryside, because when we got to the other side, we noticed that there was an explosion of tracks …tracks that made a trail by the lake, and another [trail] here, and there, and over there. Deer and squirrels and you-name-it, every animal in the countryside had come across at that particular area. We started observing our environment … and we noticed that we could tell how long it had been since something had crossed through the area. With the incredible amount of rain—it was constantly misting or raining—we could put a foot in the mud and then pull it out, and water would swirl [into the track] and it would be all muddy, and within a minute or two the edge of the footprint would begin to collapse. Within fifteen minutes [the track] was almost indistinct. The reason we paid attention to this was because we started noticing the footprints of bears.

In a couple of these [bear prints] the water was still muddy and swirling and you could see the tips of the claws. [Some of the tracks] were pretty good-sized—about the size of my hand. No instep, real rounded on the heel, just barely straight on both sides and you could see the little tips of the claws. There was a space from the end of each toe and a little claw-tip struck in the mud. I'd never studied track sign[77] ... but I'd read about it, and I thought this was pretty neat—I'd figured out how to read the track of an animal. At any rate, a couple of times we had real close encounters with bears.

After the gorge crossing, we made it to the foot of Green Monster Mountain. We needed to go up a slope, along one of the ridges, and then back to where the mine site was located. What happened was, we came onto the crest of the ridge. The crest wasn't very wide—maybe only eighty feet wide, and it dropped off very, very quickly on either side. Buster was carrying a 30.06 [caliber rifle] because we felt we might need some protection from bears. We knew there were no grizzlies on the island, just black bears and cinnamon bears [a brown phase of the black bear species]. Well, we walked, literally, to within twenty feet of one.

The wind just happened to be coming from the direction of the bear. The bear was ... sort of rocked back, leaning against a dugout or a kind of trench, sitting there scratching himself, looking around. We were almost on top of him before realizing he was there. So we got down flat on the ground, and the bear hadn't seen us. We slithered on down the slope past him and worked our way on down. After another half mile or so we came to a big wall of ice and snow, and we couldn't go over that. It was too precipitous. So we turned back, skirted around the bear, still sitting there, and made the gorge crossing again.

The next day my dad and Buster went out, and the following day we took a day off. The day after that, Buster and I tried again, but we traveled in the opposite direction. Because of heavy vegetation, it took us a long, long time to get through this particular area. There was moss growing everywhere, and the moss was real thick, like carpet, three or four inches thick. It was spongy and full of water, and trees were fallen and jumbled. It wasn't unusual to step through rotten wood [beneath the moss] and catch your foot or ankle. Buster and I were joking and talking about falling through one of these holes and finding a bear asleep underneath, and how the bear would beat the tar out of us and toss us back out because we woke him up.

Anyway, it took a while to traverse this one particular area—to go only about eight hundred to nine hundred yards. Densely foliated. Literally a jungle in there. We had a devil of a time, climbing over things and around things, through the moss and over little holes, and trying to keep from falling through jumbles of logs. Finally we got to a place where the foliage started to clear a little. A sheer rocky cliff face was on one side and Lake Josephine on the other, and we were working toward this slope, trying to get to the other end of Green Monster Mountain. We heard some kind of noise that we couldn't quite identify. We moved on a little farther, stopping every few yards, until we heard what sounded like snapping leaves and twigs. Sort of like something plodding heavily through the forest ... almost a walking movement, regular snapping, crunching, and then it would stop. We thought this was out in front of us, but we really couldn't place where the sound was coming from because it was reflected off the rocky cliff face. We looked at each other and said, 'Did you hear that?' We finally decided it was a bear and that we'd best keep our eyes open, though we couldn't see very far ahead … not more than seventy yards ahead. We pressed on and a couple of more times we heard these same plodding sounds.

Finally, we broke through the heaviest part of the vegetation and were able to come onto the slope. Off to the right … was another mountain, and about two hundred yards in that direction, was a little brown [cinnamon] bear. So we said … ah, bear, no problem, deciding that that was what we had heard. We gave the bear a wide berth—it was headed up the other mountain and that was not where we wanted to go anyway.

So we took off up the other slope. From that point, where we separated from the bear, it was probably a mile at the most [to the mine site]. It took us a little while, but then we located the site. The old trenches were overgrown. We found the opening to a tunnel, but there was a big mass of ice hanging in there, and we didn't want to go in and shake it loose. It was big enough that it could drop down and seal the tunnel and trap us in there. So we went into the trenches and explored around for quite a while, and finally I worked my way down the slope and found an area where there had been some digging—probably by the earlier expedition. We found what we were looking for and started collecting like crazy.

We had found some plastic sheet [believed left by the previous expedition], and when it began raining again we tucked this around us to keep the wind off— there was a pretty good wind running up the slope. We couldn't hear much in the way of sounds other than the wind coming off the ocean. The temperature was about fifty degrees [Fahrenheit] and with the rain we were wet and mucky and semi-miserable. We gathered up everything we could, but we didn't have enough packing materials for all that we were able to collect. So we found some skunk cabbage, the big leaves, and started wrapping the specimens in the leaves and stuffing them into our pack sacks. I estimated that we had enough [in crystals] that day to pay for the cost of the trip.

A couple of days later, Buster and Roy made a last trek to the mine site.

We departed the site late in the day, maybe 8:00 P.M., though of course it was still daylight. We were probably on site seven hours. It had taken a couple of hours to get there. So we left the site about 8:00 or 8:30 P.M., and decided the best way back was to simply retrace our steps. We headed back up the slope to the mountain ridge. The distance was about two hundred yards from the site to the ridge. We worked our way up. There were areas of trees and open areas. A line of trees was directly above us. We made it to the ridge where Buster stopped and said he had to whiz—a nature call. So I was standing there and he was making smart remarks ... and I turned to face the direction [in which] we needed to go, which was toward the west.

Now, we were standing in this little area between a snow field and vegetation, and it's all mucky and soft, and water is running off the snow, and I looked ahead of me ... and saw what looked like a footprint, just as if I had taken my boot off and put my foot into the mud and lifted it back out. But what bugged me about it was that the print was about *twice the size* of my foot! I wear about a size eight-and-a-half shoe. Well, I put my foot toward it, and looked at it, and it was twice the size of my shoe! It looked human, with an instep and five toes—a big toe, and the four little piggies that went to market and all that. A little farther ahead was another track—and not the normal distance of a human stride but nearly double that, maybe thirty to thirty-five inches. A little farther ahead was part of another one—the front half of the foot, not the back half.

By this time Buster had finished and I didn't say a word, I just pointed at the tracks. His eyes got about as wide as dinner plates. He didn't say anything, exactly, but I remember looking up and around all of a sudden, because the hair came up on the back of my neck. *The water was still running into the tracks*. The sides of the tracks hadn't yet started to collapse! Whatever was there had been there only a moment or two before us. I remember looking up, trying to see where something that size could conceal itself. Whatever it was, it had been above us, watching us, and as we came up the slope had gotten away from us—had moved away very quickly. I picked up on that right away, because we had earlier been looking at the bear tracks, trying to figure how much time had elapsed since a bear had passed by.

I could almost put both my feet into one of those tracks. At a rough guess, I'd say they were fifteen to sixteen inches long. In width, [they were] a little on the narrow side, which I found unusual ... I expected something that size to be a bit wider. The impressions were almost two inches deep. The impression of my right foot was not even half as deep. My body weight at the time was about 140 to 150 pounds, so my guess is that this thing was more than twice my weight—in the three hundred- to four hundred-pound range at least! You need to realize that, with a larger foot, the weight would be dispersed over a larger area.

The third [partial] print showed just the front of the foot touching down. It was as though [the creature] had broken into a run. We didn't see any tracks beyond the third because the texture of the area changed to moss and grass. Tracks were probably there, but I was immediately concerned with those right in front of me, in the mud.

We probably didn't say a word for a couple of minutes—we just stood there and looked around. Few things really frighten me like that, but I was dealing with something out there that I couldn't see! In my somewhat agitated state, I immediately linked the tracks to the sounds we had heard [on the previous trip] ... the crunching, the sound of regular walking. Maybe it wasn't the bear after all that we had heard ... Maybe the bear just happened to be there as we came out. Whatever this was, it had been observing us for a period of time.

During the trip back, we really didn't say much about it. We got back [to camp] about 10:00 P.M. When we told my dad about it, his reaction was sort of a 'Well, I'm not surprised' reaction, maybe because he'd been out in the woods quite a bit and I guess he had run into some unusual things from time to time. Also, you must remember that this area was relatively primitive. There was hardly anything in the way of human traffic—there were no roads, no cars, no nature settlements ... there really are no people out there, and you're going to run into things that are out of the norm.

Asked during the interview if a camera had been packed along on the expedition, Roy noted that a 35-mm camera had indeed been part of their equipment. "We just didn't want to carry it that day," he said. "We just wanted to try to get to the site. A little aside to all of this: at the cabin we were using carbide lamps for illumination, so we didn't have to worry about batteries and such. Buster [the night after discovering the tracks] was getting ready to hang his lamp outside. Rather than empty the lamps, we would hang them on a piece of rope tied outside the window. Buster had his light on and started toward the window, holding the light in front of him. He saw something in the window and threw his lamp in the air and let out a blood-curdling scream. My dad, who was in a top bunk, rolled off the bed and grabbed the rifle and was standing at the window before we even knew what had happened. Very cautiously, we opened the window—we were absolutely scared out of our wits, but of what we didn't know ... and then Buster started laughing. I said, 'What the hell's wrong with you?' And he said, 'I know what it was. I saw my own reflection in the window!'"

NOTES

74. Among the early cryptozoologists to investigate or research reports of yeti or sasquatch were Peter and Bryan Byrne, John Green, Ivan Sanderson, Tom Slick, F. Kirk Johnson, Sr., and F. Kirk Johnson, Jr., Rene Dahinden, and the Belgian zoologist, Bernard Heuvelmans.

    Heuvelmans is regarded as the "father" of modern cryptozoology and has served as president of the International Society of Cryptozoology since its founding in 1982 (P.O. Box 43070, Tucson, Arizona 85733, for additional information). He is the author of many cryptozoological works, including the classic *On the Track of Unknown Animals* (London: Rupert Hart-Davis, 1958; New York: Hill and Wang, 1959).

    For a look at the early research efforts of these and other men, the reader is directed to Loren Coleman's *Tom Slick and the Search for the Yeti* (Boston: Faber and Faber, Inc., 1989).

75. The pilot who transported the expedition members to Prince of Wales did not remain on the island. A pre-arranged pickup was agreed upon.

However, the pilot also agreed to fly over the island and watch for signal flares in the event of trouble or an early departure. Richard Jones, who was thirty-nine at the time of the expedition, died in 1982 at the age of sixty-three.

76. Though both Roy and Buster were soaked as a result of their experience at the gorge, the weather was warm enough and the men sufficiently active so that neither suffered from hypothermia. Nevertheless, Roy has acknowledged that they were "woefully unprepared" for their adventure and at times "incredibly lucky."

77. Track "sign," in this context, refers specifically to the understanding of an animal's movements by studying its tracks; but animal sign is much more. To quote wildlife writer Wilf E. Pyle in an article entitled "What Sign Means," in the January 1987 issue of the magazine *Fur-Fish-Game*: "Sign is the record or chronicle of the animal's activities. It can be paw and claw marks, but also scats and urine spots, loafing sites and bedding areas. It can be travel routes through grasses and low bush, remains of a kill or the disturbed earth of a life and death struggle."

Limbo

I often wonder just how many people know that both people and things have been and still are being reported as vanishing ...

—Ivan T. Sanderson

Mysterious blasts have been occurring ... for many years, and there are legends of "phantom artillery" going back several centuries.

—John A. Keel

Chapter Thirteen:

Trains, Planes, Wrecker Balls, and Bulldozers

S trange disappearances—as opposed to vanishings that can be explained rationally—have a profound, lasting effect on the human psyche. Put another way: they disturb the hell out of us!

Consider, for example, the disappearance of famed pilot Amelia Earhart.[78] She vanished in the South Pacific on July 2, 1937, while attempting to be the first woman to fly around the world. A full-scale search turned up no trace of her aircraft, even though the rough coordinates were known. The loss stunned her adoring public so much that efforts to locate the plane have continued until as recently as 1989.

That Earhart's celebrity status had much to do with the notoriety of, and public concern about, this instance there is little doubt. Perhaps an underlying reason is that the disappearance was hardly an isolated event. Each year thousands of people and objects dematerialize and are never seen or heard from again.

In early 1970, people living near the town of Salem in Marion County, Illinois, were confronted with a rash of unexplained hog disappearances. During early June of that year, Deputy Sheriff G. M. Walker reported that twenty-four hogs had vanished without a clue within a three-week period. Furthermore, said Walker, "many more [disappearances] than that" had occurred during the previous three months. The best he or anyone else could do by way of explanation was to speculate that the hogs had been swiped by well-equipped livestock thieves. Perhaps someone was planning a giant pork chop roast?

An inoperative earth-mover sitting on the property of the J. T. Evanick Co. in Scranton, Pennsylvania was apparently duck soup for the forces of dematerialization, despite the vehicle's dead engine. According to the Associated Press, corporation officials took four days to report the bulldozer's disappearance "because they just could not believe it." The 'dozer' weighed about twenty-five tons and had been out of operation ever since its engine was accidentally filled with sand. The incident occurred during January 1971.

On February 20, 1971, the news media reported that the Coast Guard had taken under tow the Danish yacht *Frilo*, found drifting in the Atlantic Ocean. The *Frilo*, owned and piloted by fifty-one-year-old Bjorn Christian Lohr, had departed Denmark on December 31, 1970 on a solo Atlantic crossing. Although the *Frilo* was undamaged and, in fact, quite seaworthy when it was discovered, Lohr was nowhere to be found.

It isn't every day that police have the opportunity to investigate a reported missing cannon, but in March 1971, Centralia, Illinois authorities did just that. The cannon, a five hundred-pound Civil War piece, had been hauled from Centralia's Elmwood Park, and police speculated that the culprit was a winch-trucking cannon-bandit. However, no truck tracks were reported at the site and the cannon, so far as is known, has never been recovered.

At about the same time as the cannon disappearance, a mysterious force tore the porch from a vacant house two miles west of Centralia and knocked the chimney from the roof. Again, authorities speculated that a phantom winch truck was involved.

During the early morning hours of March 18, 1971, a railroad switching engine was mysteriously transported from its berth in the Chicago and Northwestern Railway switching yard at Crystal Lake, Illinois to a point twenty-seven miles away, where it rammed into a standing suburban train. Damage was extensive to the parked train, and a crewman asleep in the suburban suffered minor injuries. A rail official told reporters that in order to move the switching engine from the yard and out to the branch line, several switches had to be pulled and a main line crossed. The spokesperson was unable to explain how the maneuvers could be executed without alerting the necessary railroad personnel all along the route.

On June 28, 1971, a farmer living near Dobbiaco, Italy discovered that an old five-ton iron bridge had vanished completely from an isolated part of his property. Police suggested that the structure had been dismantled and hauled away by some obsessed bridge-lover. The farmer wondered how such a person would ever have found the bridge, considering its remote location.

According to an account in the April 1971 *Pursuit*[79], you can talk to plants and sing to plants—just don't open a knife in their presence. The writer of the report (an unidentified male) claimed that he was trying to cut a patch of wild sassafras plants when his pocketknife suddenly vanished. He said the knife literally twisted in his hand as he applied pressure to the wood. "There was a sort of blurring effect, but I didn't really see it go. Nor did I hear any sound of impact on the dry leaves or piled dead brush. It was just gone."

Months later, after repeatedly searching the area for the knife, the object reappeared. Said the owner: "I swear that I saw my knife while I was still some twenty-odd feet away. It was lying on the bare soil, about eighteen inches from the bush I'd been cutting when it vanished." The blade did not have a speck of rust on it. (In a footnote, a *Pursuit* editor wrote: "We know this gentleman well enough to state positively that he is not a liar; his account must therefore be taken at face value.")

November 22, 1972 is known in Naples, Italy as the night the windshields vanished. During the course of that evening some forty windshields disappeared from vehicles parked throughout the city. Police could offer no reason for the mass theft, let alone explain how it was accomplished.

New love is always a difficult road to travel, but for Mrs. Mirfat Ahmed Shihata and her husband, it proved impassable. On March 28, 1973, the bride of only four months vanished—literally swallowed by the earth. According to the Middle East News Agency, twenty-year-old Mrs. Shihata was walking with her husband along a street in Alexandria, Egypt when she dropped into a crevice that had abruptly opened in the roadway and then closed just as quickly. Rescue workers summoned to the scene dug down ten yards without finding a trace of her.

In mid-April 1973, Mrs. David Griffon, of Newton, Utah returned home from a three-day trip to find her barn missing. While everything else was exactly as Mrs. Griffon had left it, she couldn't find her barn anywhere. The incident was reported to police, who were of no help at all.

Loran Dowling, owner of the Dowling Construction Company, Indianapolis, Indiana, was no doubt a perplexed owner when he learned in July 1973 that the company's five-ton wrecker ball had vanished. When last seen, the sphere had been suspended from a crane cable about two hundred feet above the ground. Workers reported it missing.

In July 1974, Air Force Lieutenant W. T. Day and Flight Officer D. R. Steward took off in a single-engine aircraft on a routine patrol over the Arabian desert. They never returned. The following day a search party found their plane parked on the desert sand; the aircraft was still in working order and there was gasoline in the tanks. The footprints of the two fliers were visible in the sand. The tracks led away from the aircraft for a short way, then simply stopped.

According to journalist John Keel, weather vanes were vanishing with regularity from the roofs and chimneys of buildings throughout New England during the early years of the 1970s. Homeowners in New Hampshire, Vermont, and Massachusetts were all victimized by vane vandals who, Keel proposed, flew over an intended target in a bright orange helicopter (reported in some cases), lassoed the vane, then yanked it free as they flew past. Authorities of course were unable to trace the helicopter, and Keel himself admitted that "your average helicopter owner can find easier legal ways to make a dollar."

In January 1976, a five hundred-pound tree stump vanished from a fire company parking lot in Ridgeway, Illinois where it had been uprooted to make way for a small building. The stump reappeared a couple of nights later, only to vanish a second time, according to a United Press International account dated February 9, 1976. It didn't stay lost. In the course of its meanderings, the stump appeared and disappeared in a garage, in a van, on the front lawns of several homes, and finally on the front steps of the home of Mayor J. B. Holmes. The mayor's wife, Iona, said she tied a red ribbon to the stump and then it vanished again. "It was out front of our house for two nights," she said. "We didn't see it leave."

On October 22, 1978 a twenty-year-old Australian named Frederick Valentich was on an extended training flight in a single-engine Cessna when he radioed an odd message to air traffic controllers in Melbourne. According to the Associated Press and other news sources, Valentich said his aircraft was being followed by a brightly-lit object at an altitude of about forty-five hundred feet. The time was 5:06 A.M. EDT. Air traffic controllers radioed back that they were unable to detect other traffic in the area below five thousand feet.

Valentich replied: "It has four bright lights— appear to be landing lights. Aircraft has just passed over me about one thousand feet above."

Control: "Can you identify the aircraft?"

Valentich: "It isn't an aircraft. It's ..."

There was silence for about two minutes, then Valentich's voice returned. "Melbourne, it's approaching from due east toward me. It seems to be playing some sort of game. Flying at a speed I cannot estimate. It is flying past. It is a long shape. Cannot identify more than that ... coming for me right now. It seems to be stationary. I'm orbiting and the thing is orbiting on top of me also. It has a green light and sort of metallic light on the outside."

The young pilot next reported that his aircraft engine was failing, after which controllers reported they heard over the radio a strange metallic sound, then only silence. An extensive, week-long search by the Australian Air Force turned up no trace of the Cessna or its pilot. Frederick Valentich had vanished from the face of the Earth.

Not all disappearances occur within the Earth's atmosphere. Some occur in the darkness of space. On December 10, 1979, Satcom III, a communications satellite owned by the RCA Corporation, was launched into space toward an orbital path 22,300 miles above the Pacific. The satellite never reached orbit. Personnel monitoring the launch watched, disbelieving, as the fifty million dollar device vanished from their tracking screens. A two-month search followed, conducted jointly by the RCA Earth Station in Vernon Valley, New Jersey, the

National Aeronautics and Space Administration (NASA), and the North American Air Defense Command (NORAD). The search, however, failed to turn up any sign of Satcom III.[80]

On October 13, 1993, workmen at a construction site along Interstate 79, near Erie, Pennsylvania, reported the disappearance of a steamroller weighing several tons. The steamroller had been parked overnight and, according to news accounts, police and road crewmen could uncover no clue as to how it had been taken, or why.

Sometimes things mysteriously appear as well as disappear. In September 1978 thousands of feet of fishing line presumably fell from the sky over Greensburg, Ohio. According to a September 24 report in the St. Louis *Post–Dispatch*, a knot of fishing line was found snagged on a bush on the property of John Wright. However, when Wright tried to remove it, he discovered that the line seemed to have no end. Neighbors with fishing reels assisted in collecting the stuff, and roughly one thousand feet were hauled in—filling eight reels—before the line broke and floated away. Wright's co-worker at an automotive plant, Ken Corasmun, tracked the line visually for some two thousand feet before losing sight of it. The line simply continued on and on, vanishing into the sky.

A similar episode involving "sky-lines" occurred during the summer of 1970 over Caldwell, New Jersey.[81] A half-dozen lines were reported, stretched taut at thirty- to fifty-degree angles across the sky with neither end in sight. One line was reported in place for an entire month, even during heavy winds and at least one electrical storm. Samples given to Du Pont were analyzed and determined to be a kind of nylon.

Observers reported that the lines vanished to a point of invisibility, even when traced with powerful binoculars. In one instance, four boys spent an entire hour hauling in a line after one end of it fell during the night. However, the line snagged and broke before the other end was ever in sight.

As a boy of twelve, I can recall spinning the cardboard back of a writing tablet down a flight of stairs and watching it fall behind an ironing board standing against a wall. The landing at the base of the stairway was a space about four feet square. The only objects in that area were the ironing board and a small sewing box. When I moved the board to retrieve the cardboard, it wasn't there. Nor was it under the sewing box.

Tonight before crawling under the covers take a count of your family members and a quick look around. Something, or someone, may be missing.

NOTES

78. A brief, final radio transmission preceded Amelia Earhart's disappearance on July 2, 1937. The message was: "We are on the line of position 157 dash 133; we are running north and south." Earhart and her copilot-navigator, Fred Noonan, were at the time (about 8:44 A.M.) bound for Howland Island in the Pacific where they were to make contact with a waiting Coast Guard cutter, the *Itasca*. Radio monitors located Earhart's twin-engine Lockheed Electra within

one hundred miles of Howland Island. The Navy dispatched seven ships from Hawaii, including the aircraft carrier *USS Lexington*. All ninety-eight of the carrier's planes were put into the search. However, many of the pilots reportedly flew with a bad attitude. The disappearance, they believed, was a publicity stunt.

A close friend of Earhart's, aviatrix Jacqueline Cochran (see Chapter One), was asked by Amelia's husband, George Putnam, to try to locate his wife. Cochran, who was believed by Earhart to have extrasensory perception, had located other missing planes. In an autobiography, *The Stars At Noon*, Cochran said she told Putnam that Amelia was alive. She gave a specific location for the aircraft and identified two nearby vessels—one of them the *Itasca* (a vessel of which she had no prior knowledge). Despite this, no trace of the aircraft was ever found.

79. "Into Thin Air—And Out Again," *Pursuit*, April 1971, pp. 31–32.
80. "$50 Million Vanishes In Thin Air," *Pursuit*, Spring 1980, p. 77.
81. "Sky-Lines," *Pursuit*, January 1971, p. 6.

Chapter Fourteen

Things That Go Boom in the Night

There is a part of the Earth's atmosphere—extending from about thirty miles to roughly 250 miles in altitude—which acts as a kind of "mirror" in the sky. This section of sky is called the ionosphere and it is a concentration of electrically charged particles. The particle concentration reflects radio waves so a signal can be "bounced" and transmitted a much greater distance over the curved planetary surface. On April 26, 1973, the ionosphere briefly vanished: that is, for some unknown reason it ceased to reflect radio waves sent up from the ground!

The events leading up to the ionosphere's disappearance were described in an August 18, 1973 article by Associated Press science writer Frank Carey. On April 26, the second-largest earthquake to hit the Hawaiian Islands in a century rocked the coastal town of Hilo, on the island of Hawaii. The quake registered 6.2 on the Richter scale and was equal in intensity to a quake that, in December 1973, leveled the Nicaraguan capital of Managua[82]. The epicenter of the Hawaiian quake was located twelve miles offshore and some twenty-five miles below the ocean surface. Authorities noted that only the quake's distance from shore prevented extensive damage or loss of human life. Even so, the tremor rocked buildings, triggered landslides, and even affected the city of Honolulu, some two hundred miles northwest of Hawaii Island.

Dr. Augustine S. Furumoto of the University of Hawaii told Carey that the ground continued to vibrate two hours after the initial shock was recorded. "[The tremor] should have died off in about a half-hour or forty-five minutes," Furumoto said. "We're still trying to figure out the reason for this."

Even more perplexing was the disappearance of the ionosphere, which, it was soon realized, was in some way related to the earthquake. According to Carey, when the quake hit, University of Hawaii researchers were experimenting with a broadcast system that enabled them to detect the presence of airborne Rayleigh waves—pressure waves that precede an earthquake. Scientists have long been aware of ground-transmitted Rayleigh waves, but at the time they had only recently become aware of an airborne, or acoustic, variety. It was hoped that accurate detection of the acoustic waves, by means of special radio signals, would give seismologists a way to accurately forecast tsunami (tidal wave) activity.

Furumoto and his colleagues were scanning for these waves when they discovered that their signals were no longer coming back; the ionosphere's electrically charged "mirror" was no longer reflecting radio waves. This was almost an hour before the occurrence of the earthquake. At about the same time, United States Navy personnel were encountering difficulty with their own radio transmissions.

Affected was the Navy's sophisticated Omega Navigational System, a pattern of long-wavelength radio signals used to guide seagoing ships. Furumoto told Carey that the Omega system "began drifting and not making any sense. It hit maximum drift just about the time of the occurrence of the quake and then began to recover." This was all "too much like Buck Rogers," he added. "We have no explanation for it yet."

The disappearance of the ionosphere, albeit temporary, and the peculiarly prolonged nature of the Hawaiian earthquake, are atmospheric and seismological mysteries of no small importance. Nonetheless, they are only part of a larger body of occurrences that have long baffled earth scientists.

On Saturday, June 22, 1974, a series of "mystery shakes" was reported by news wire services on the West Coast. The tremors occurred along a seventy-mile stretch of Southern California, ranging from "Camarillo to the north through the Los Angeles area to Whittier and west to the sea." Throughout this area residents experienced "jouncings, tremors, bumps and booms." The bizarre goings-on were reported to authorities at various times and in various locations on June 20 and 21, 1974. California Institute of Technology (Cal Tech) Seismological Laboratory scientists, who were questioned about the tremors, insisted that no quake activity had been recorded. This assertion failed to satisfy dogmatic homeowners who maintained that the weird booms and quivers were all too apparent. Considering California's earthquake-prone reputation, one can easily understand their anxiety.

An unidentified Cal Tech spokesman later observed that the tremors were similar to a series of mystery quakes that shook the Los Angeles area in January 1930. He also noted that in 1931, two Cal Tech researchers dubbed such phenomena "pseudo-seisms"—meaning the quakes and booms were not natural occurrences. Indeed, the 1930 tremors were finally attributed to naval gunfire at sea—the theory being that extremely loud gunfire creates shock waves that enter the stratosphere, bounce back, and strike the earth some distance from their point of origin. The bounce-back theory reportedly originated with Charles R. Richter, the scientist for whom the open-ended Richter scale is named. Unfortunately, the United States Navy had a problem with this explanation: a spokesman said the mystery booms did not occur at, or around, the time of any known firing of large guns at sea.

The Navy, however, was not the only branch of the armed forces to receive blame. Personnel at Vandenberg AFB were accused of test-firing missiles which set off the booms and tremors. The Air Force denied this, insisting that no missiles were tested on June 20 or 21, 1974.

This was, in fact, the second time in several months that Air Force personnel were blamed for causing an atmospheric disturbance. On March 20, 1974, at about 3:15 A.M., a series of mystery booms rocked the San Francisco Bay area. According to accounts in both the San Francisco *Chronicle* and *Examiner*, police received a dozen phone calls from sleepy residents "who wanted to know if the city had been hit by another earthquake." San Rafael, California police received approximately fifty telephone calls, while residents of San Mateo and Marin counties likewise reported early morning booms. Questioned about the blasts, city and county officials immediately blamed the Air Force, citing "sonic booms" triggered by high speed jet aircraft.

To clarify, a sonic boom is the sound of a shock wave formed at the nose of an aircraft moving at supersonic speeds. The shock wave strikes the ground and causes an explosive sound. Military jets, as a rule, are prohibited from flying at supersonic speeds over populated areas, and personnel at Beale AFB of course denied the allegation.

Odd seismic and atmospheric disturbances are recurrent phenomena in many parts of the world—they date back at least several centuries. In 1784, subterranean "thunder" was heard at Guanajuato, Mexico, but with no accompanying tremor.[83] In 1805 near what is today Great Falls, Montana, Captains Meriwether Lewis and William Clark, on their western expedition, heard inexplicable cannon-like booming sounds.[84] In April 1817, strange aerial "howling noises" were reported during an earthquake at Palermo, Italy.[85]

On March 20, 1822, in the village of Babino Polje, on Mljet Island in the Adriatic Sea, sounds resembling "the reports of a cannon" shook doors and windows. The booms were at first attributed to large guns fired by seagoing warships. However, the booms were repeated "four, ten and even a hundred times in a day, at all hours and in all weathers." The noise continued until February 1824, then ceased before resuming again in September of the same year. This time the booms continued on and off until March 1825.[86]

In 1829, on a calm, clear day, members of an expedition to what is today New South Wales, Australia heard "cannon-like" noises.[87] In 1839, at Comrie,

Scotland, a "barrage" of cannon-like sounds commenced and continued on and off until October 1841. A total of 250 blasts were reported during the two-year period, many accompanied by tremors.[88]

These strange shock waves, in more recent years, have been given a name: "skyquakes." On October 24, 1973, residents of Pennsylvania, Maryland, West Virginia, Ohio and Indiana were treated to a skyquake that rattled windows over a wide area. The quake occurred at about 9:00 P.M., and newspaper offices, police departments, and radio and television stations were deluged with calls from concerned homeowners.

Scientists speculated that a large meteor entering the atmosphere may have been the source of the disturbance. However, Air National Guard personnel at Harrisburg (Pennsylvania) International Airport and officers at the Naval Observatory in Washington, D.C., said no meteors had been reported. NASA's Goddard Space Flight Center at Greenbelt, Maryland was also unable to account for the boom.

Three days later, on October 27, 1973, Florida was jolted by a rare earthquake that shook buildings in four counties. A story in the *St. Petersburg Times* noted that some geologists had questioned whether Florida could have earthquakes "because its limestone foundation tends to cushion shocks." However, according to the National Earthquake Information Service, at least seven quakes have been felt in the state since the 1870s.

A series of powerful skyquakes rocked the East Coast in December 1977, leaving geologists and local authorities guessing as usual. The first quake occurred on December 2, with others following at intervals over the next six weeks. They were recorded

on microbarographs at Columbia University's Lamont-Doherty Geological Observatory at Palisades,
New York. They were also recorded on instruments
in South Carolina, where skyquakes in the
Charleston area knocked out windows and shook
buildings. Curiously, there were no reports of
skyquakes being heard anywhere between New Jersey and South Carolina.

Dr. William L. Donn, a geologist at the Lamont-
Doherty Observatory, told Walter Sullivan of the *New
York Times*[89] that the disturbances were acoustic pressure waves and not ground-transmitted shock waves.
He said he doubted the booms were caused by supersonic aircraft, noting that not even a formation of jets
simultaneously breaking the sound barrier could produce the observed effect. In fact, Donn said that when
the first blast occurred, he suspected the cause was a
meteor entering the atmosphere, but when additional
skyquakes occurred, and in fact repeated for several
weeks, he was forced to rule out the idea.

Sullivan reported that the microbarographs used
to record the blasts were designed to register microscopic changes in barometric pressure, "such as those
generated by distant nuclear explosions." According to
Donn, the recorded "signature" of the skyquakes bore
no resemblance to a nuclear explosion. He suggested,
instead, that methane gas may have bubbled up from
oil-gas deposits under the continental shelf and ignited after rising into the atmosphere. How the gas could
have ignited was open to debate, and Donn himself
seemed to have little faith in the explanation. One
notion was that the gas was sparked by static electric-
ity. Another was that it was torched by a passing aircraft—though of course the frightened pilot or crew
would have noticed and, assuming they themselves

were not blown to bits, reported the incident—and there had been no such reports.

The exploding gas explanation was also proposed by an environmental engineering scientist and associate professor of civil engineering at Colorado State University, Dr. Stanley Klemetson.[90] Instead of methane gas from offshore deposits, Klemetson suggested methane or hydrogen gas rising from submerged garbage and treated waste-sludge deposits. To add weight to his theory, Klemetson pointed out that the blasts were occurring near large cities where garbage was being dumped offshore. His theory, however, failed to take into account the historical component noted earlier: skyquakes were reported on the continent during the earliest days of European exploration and settlement, when there were no large deposits of garbage.

Whatever their source, the skyquakes that began on December 2, 1977 were heard all along the New Jersey coastline. A Surf City police officer named Frank Keicher told the *New York Times* that the December 2 blast "was like a clap of thunder, but there was no light preceding it."[91] The boom vibrated the glass door of his home and sent residents running into the streets. Keicher, a former member of the United States Navy, compared the blast to the discharge of eight-inch naval guns. When asked about this, a Navy spokesperson issued the usual denial.

The Pentagon also denied knowledge of the quakes. Though later, in March 1978, the Defense Department issued a rather suspicious claim that some of the blasts were caused by experimental supersonic aircraft. Why the aircraft were flown offshore and not in the usual top-secret test areas was never explained. In view of the public uproar caused by the skyquakes, substantial pressure may have been exerted by upper echelon officials to find a solution—any solution—to the mystery.

In a brief published review of the skyquake occurrences of December 1977 and January 1978, Dr. David Rind, an associate of William Donn's at the Lamont-Doherty Geological Observatory, was highly critical of the various explanations.[92] He declared that none "can stand even the most minimal scrutiny," and offered a rather astonishing alternative: that skyquakes may be natural phenomena occurring in some other, perhaps parallel, dimension or reality and which are *occasionally bleeding over into our own*.

"Perhaps," Rind suggested, "these mysterious 'skyquakes' are a common feature of the reality which Carlos Castaneda[93] has described in his five books. If so, it is then the height of irrationality to try and rope into our preconceived view of the world something [an explanation] which will not fit; it becomes as ridiculous as it would be for savages to attempt to explain electric lights, or even for psychologists to attempt to explain abstract geometric patterns ..."

If Rind is correct, this represents a sort of reverse of events described in the previous chapter: Instead of mysterious disappearances, the skyquakes represent a form of energy from an entirely different realm— something arriving from out of limbo. What's more, whether one agrees with Rind's conjecture or not, it remains true that no one has yet been able to offer a truly credible explanation for the skyquakes, so his suggestion is worth at least as much as any other.

Meanwhile, we can be certain that the mysterious quakes, quirks, and things that go boom in the night will continue to be heard, at odd intervals and at various locations around the globe—and perhaps even next in your neighborhood.

NOTES

82. Roughly five thousand deaths were recorded following the December 23, 1972 earthquake in Managua, Nicaragua. The quake registered 6.2 on the Richter scale.

83. *Philosophical Magazine*, January 1900, pp. 49, 58.

84. *Nature*, March 26, 1896, p. 487.

85. Report of The 24th Meeting of The British Association for The Advancement of Science, Vol. 24 (1854), p. III.

86. *American Journal of Science and Arts*, February 1826, pp. 10, 377.

87. *Nature*, July 29, 1909, p. 127.

88. *The Edinburgh New Philosophical Journal*, October 1841–April 1842, pp. 106–109.

89. "Atmospheric Blasts over Atlantic Region Remain a Mystery to the Experts," *New York Times*, January 13, 1978, p. B5.

90. "Mystery Booms In Atlantic Bring Spate of Speculation," *Denver Post*, December 24, 1977.

91. *New York Times*, January 13, 1978, p. A1.

92. David Rind, "Skyquakes—And Separate Realities," *Pursuit*, Spring 1978, pp. 51–54.

93. Carlos Castaneda, author of numerous books, including *Journey to Ixlan: Lessons of don Juan* (1972), and *The Power of Silence: Further Teachings of don Juan* (1987). Castaneda's books focus largely on Yaqui medicine man don Juan, who describes an alternate magical reality.

Chapter Fifteen

Lost is the *Light Heart*

Thomas L. Gatch, Jr. was a Korean war veteran. He was also a colonel in the Army Reserve, a bachelor, and a balloonist. In February 1974, he set off on a transatlantic voyage in a specially designed high-altitude balloon. Four days later he was missing, and despite an extensive air-sea search and the efforts of his family, no trace has ever been found.

Tom was forty-eight when the mooring ropes were cast free and his lightweight gondola, carried aloft by ten white helium-filled spheres, ascended over the fields and forests of southeastern Pennsylvania. It was not his first time in a balloon: he had joined the ranks of American aeronauts in 1971, and soon thereafter began work on Project Light Heart.

The idea behind the project was to build a "clean energy" device and demonstrate to the world that, without polluting energy sources, a person could fly rapidly to remote parts of the globe. However, this was only part of the dream. The romantic, spirited soul in Tom recognized a chance to make history—to enter the record books as the first aeronaut to cross the North Atlantic.

The craft *Light Heart* launched from Harrisburg, Pennsylvania International Airport at 7:29 P.M. on February 18, 1974. The flight plan was simple: climb to an altitude of thirty-nine thousand feet, where the balloon would enter the powerful air current known as the jet stream, and ride that current east to Europe—hopefully to France or southern Spain. The voyage was to last about three days, but Gatch was prepared for much longer—carrying with him a ten-day supply of astronaut food rations. In addition, he outfitted the gondola with a radio transceiver, flares, reflective mirrors, a strobe light, and an emergency "beeper" transmitter. The balloonist even included a cot for in-flight sleeping, as well as a parachute and an inflatable life raft. The gondola itself was covered with a reflective material easily detected by radar and was equipped with pontoons in the event the *Light Heart* was forced down at sea.

Tom Gatch planned for every conceivable possibility; but despite his well laid plans, the flight went awry almost at the start. After being airborne for only seventy-six minutes, one of the ten balloons burst with a "loud noise" and draped itself over a gondola porthole, partially obscuring Gatch's view. He was able to compensate by siphoning liquid ballast from the gondola. He radioed that his altitude after adjusting was about 33,550 feet.

According to news accounts at the time, the balloonist also reported that his three portholes became "slightly iced over." However, the internal temperature of the gondola was a "comfortable" forty degrees Fahrenheit, with all life-support systems working well. The *Light Heart*'s airspeed was approximately 140 miles per hour.

The loss of the helium sphere and the resulting loss of altitude greatly affected the heading of the *Light Heart*. The gondola and its passenger were shifted to the southern edge of the jet stream, where it was located by radar at John F. Kennedy International Airport in New York as approximately one hundred miles east-southeast of Bermuda. This was at 2:44 A.M., Tuesday, February 19. Two days later, the crew of a freighter reported seeing the *Light Heart* still farther south, at mid-Atlantic, and then it was never seen again.

The Atlantic region off the southern United States has long been regarded as a place where sailing vessels disappear all too routinely. Since the advent of manned flight, aircraft have frequently been lost— or have encountered odd navigational problems— over this place, which ancient mariners called the Sargasso Sea.

A common early myth about the Sargasso Sea concerned a "graveyard of ships" where sailing vessels became hopelessly entangled in the masses of sargasso grass, or gulfweed, found floating in these waters. The ships remained entangled until they rotted and sank, or so the legend went. Another early legend concerned "demons" lurking in the waters surrounding the many—literally hundreds—of coral islands which make up the Bermuda Islands. Four and a half centuries ago, no one wanted to venture near these islands for fear of disturbing the demons.[94] Today, thanks to the writer Vincent Gaddis, this entire area is known as the Bermuda Triangle—a name that has become nearly synonymous with mystery and that, for some, evokes a powerful superstitious dread. [95]

The Bermuda Triangle is said to encompass a portion of the Atlantic Ocean from the area of Norfolk, Virginia, out to the Bermuda Islands and on down to the Tropic of Cancer and a little beyond—to the neighborhood of Cuba, Haiti, and Puerto Rico, and back up to the area of the Bahamas and southern Florida. It is not really a "triangle" but a vast, essentially borderless, region. Ivan Sanderson described the area as a large "lozenge," and speculated that it was but one of ten such zones found equally spaced around the globe—five in the northern hemisphere and five in the southern. He eventually suggested that there might actually be twelve zones—the original ten plus one at each pole. Ivan's theory (and it must be emphasized that it was never more than a theory) was that these areas are the locus of powerful, anomalous electromagnetic and gravitational phenomena that become active occasionally, and only briefly, altering the immediate area of space and time. In other words, a door opens, then closes, onto elsewhere or *elsewhen*.

The worst of these zones is of course the Bermuda Triangle, although an area of the Pacific Ocean between Japan and the Mariana Islands, some 250 miles south of the Japanese island of Honshu, is said to be a close second. Popularly known as the "Devil's Sea," the place is heavily traveled and the disappearance of ships and planes here is not uncommon. The Devil's Sea lies between thirty and forty degrees North, while the Bermuda Triangle is found in nearly the same latitude—between roughly twenty-five and forty degrees North. Midway between these two areas—also at thirty and forty degrees North—is the Mediterranean Sea, which Sanderson believed was another of his twelve "vile vortices," as he came to call them. These three were the best known of the twelve zones described by Ivan in various articles and in his popular book *Invisible Residents*.[96]

To be sure, many, if not most, of the disappearances in these locations are due almost certainly to natural occurrences—storms, squalls, or freak tidal conditions that sink ships and force aircraft down into turbulent seas. Still other disappearances—those involving surface vessels, and especially smaller boats such as yachts, sloops or schooners—can be attributed to modern day piracy or the actions of drug runners at sea. Expensive pleasure craft are an inviting target for the lawless, and there are many such boats sailing the waters off south Florida. The United States Coast Guard, as well as naval and police authorities, have waged a valiant war against crime on the high seas, but for all their efforts they are able to make no more than a dent.

This still leaves a sizable body of disappearances which, on the surface, appear rather mysterious. Many of these tales have been repeated time and again, with one writer borrowing from another without really bothering to check the available facts.

A striking example is the story of the "lost patrol," the five United States Navy TBM Avenger torpedo bombers that vanished on December 5, 1945. The story has been repeated so often that anyone familiar with this type of literature is already well aware of the details. However, over the years careful researchers such as Robert J. Durant[97] and Larry Kusche[98] have demonstrated that the original account is largely a work of fiction.

In the original story, written by Allan W. Eckert and published in the April 1962 issue of *American Legion Magazine*, the flight leader is said to have transmitted the following radio message: "Everything is wrong ... strange ... We can't be sure of any direction. Even the ocean doesn't look as it should." However, according to Durant, who in 1971 visited the Bureau of Naval Personnel in Washington, D.C., where he studied at length the Navy's "bulging" file, nothing like that message ever appeared in the Navy report. An accurate transcript of Flight 19's radio messages is documented in Larry Kusche's book, *The Bermuda Triangle Mystery—Solved*. According to Kusche, the flight leader, Lieutenant Charles Caroll Taylor, began radioing that the flight was lost or disoriented fewer than two hours after takeoff. The flight was made up almost entirely of student aviators. Taylor radioed: "Both my compasses are out ... I am over land, but it's broken [land]. I'm sure I'm in the [Florida] Keys, but I don't know how far down and I don't know how to get to Fort Lauderdale."[99] Later, Taylor was overheard to transmit to the rest of the squadron: "When [the] first man gets down to ten gallons of gas we will all land in the water together. Does everyone understand that?"

Stories that a flying boat vanished while attempting a rescue of the TBMs are similarly misleading. Available information suggests that the aircraft, a Martin Mariner—a type of machine with a reputation for being unreliable—burst into flames shortly after takeoff from the Banana River Naval Air Station. Oil and debris believed to be from the Mariner were later located by a tanker crew.

In 1974, members of a Key West treasure hunting group located an aircraft—possibly an Avenger—

lying in twenty-five feet of water some twenty miles from Key West. No serial numbers from the aircraft were available, though a Navy investigation was reportedly begun.[100] The outcome of the investigation, if any, was never made public. More recently, other Avenger aircraft were discovered in Florida waters. However, the serial numbers—clearly filmed with an underwater camera and nationally televised—did not match those of Flight 19.

That all five aircraft went down at sea after running out of fuel is evident from Taylor's radio messages. Nevertheless, a five-day search spanning some 250,000 square miles failed to turn up any sign of the missing Avengers or crew.

The *Light Heart*, too, almost certainly went down at sea, though once again an extensive air-sea search failed to turn up a single clue. News reports at the time said radio signals from the balloonist were received by the Azores Islands radio station late on February 19, 1974. Two days later, Thursday, February 21, the crew of a Liberian freighter, registered under the name *Ore Meridian*, reported seeing the balloon. This placed the *Light Heart* about one thousand miles west of the Canary Islands, or somewhere over the Mid-Atlantic Ridge just east of the Sargasso Sea.

Around the same time, people on Puerto de la Cruz in the Canary Islands observed an object which they believed was the *Light Heart*. According to a United Press International account, "hundreds of tourists and natives reported seeing a bluish-white ball at about nine thousand feet." Officials clearly doubted that it was Gatch, and went so far as to suggest that it was, instead, "an optical illusion caused by rain."

Expectations that Gatch would materialize in the Spanish Sahara never bore fruit. Neither did efforts made by the United States Navy and various civilian groups that searched ninety-five thousand square miles of the mid-Atlantic without finding a trace.

Following the *Light Heart*'s disappearance, Tom's two sisters, Eleanor Hoaglan of Rochester, Minnesota, and Nancy Svien of Minneapolis, along with a niece, Jocklyn Armstrong of Washington, D.C., posted a ten thousand dollar reward for information leading to the aeronaut's whereabouts. Nineteen years later there was still no word.

"We received calls from all over," Mrs. Svien said during a long distance phone conversation in mid-June 1993. The calls came to Tom's home in Alexandria, Virginia, where the sisters remained for a full month following his disappearance. None of the calls, including those from Lloyd's of London, and from a far-flung network of ham radio operators, offered any clue as to the whereabouts of the *Light Heart* or the fate of its pilot.

Mrs. Svien's sister, Eleanor Hoaglan, who spoke from her home in Rochester, said the closely knit family did everything they could think of to try to locate the missing aeronaut. While Mrs. Svien traveled to the Canary Islands to investigate reports on Puerto de la Cruz, Mrs. Hoaglan tried another approach by visiting an expert in ESP at the Edgar Cayce Foundation for Extra-Sensory Research in Virginia Beach, Virginia. The efforts of the two sisters turned up no new information, and after all these years, Mrs. Hoaglan said, "There is just nothing, nothing, nothing."

Outside of his family, Tom Gatch had many friends and admirers. A chapter devoted to Tom appears in a book written by retired Major General John C. McWhorter, Jr., who was a classmate of Tom's at the United States Military Academy at West Point, Class of 1946. Currently residing in Kerrville, Texas, General McWhorter grew up in Edinburg, Texas and entered West Point in 1943. He served in the United States Army for thirty years, including eleven years overseas with service in both Korea and Vietnam. He also served in a research and development unit participating in the nuclear tests at Eniwetok and the Nevada Test Site, and later taught Engineering Mechanics at West Point.

General McWhorter is a graduate of the Army Command and General Staff College at Fort Leavenworth, Kansas (honor graduate of his class), and the Industrial College of the Armed Forces at Fort McNair, Washington, D.C. He served as Director, Transportation and Services, Office of the Deputy Chief of Staff, Logistics, Department of the Army, and later as Deputy J-4 for Strategic Mobility, Joint Chiefs of Staff. Retired in 1976, his book highlights the history and exploits of the graduating members of the West Point Class of 1946.[101] The chapter on Tom is prefaced with the note: "Thomas Leigh Gatch, Jr ... Lost in a balloon over the Atlantic, last sighted February, 21 1974 about 1,000 miles west of the Canary Islands, aged 48 years."

With the General's kind permission I include a portion of his chronicle of Tom Gatch:

Tom came to West Point from a long and illustrious military family tradition. His grandfather, Robert B. Dashiell, graduated from the Naval Academy in the 1880s. His uncle, General Julian S. Hatcher, was also an Annapolis graduate, but transferred into the Army in 1909. Tom's father, Vice Admiral Thomas L. Gatch, gained fame in World War II as the skipper of the battleship *South Dakota*, also known as "Battleship X" in the decisive Battle of the Coral Sea. Tom was born in Annapolis, Maryland, September 13, 1925. He graduated from Woodrow Wilson High School in Washington, D.C.

One of Tom's roommates recalls that his plebe year was reminiscent of the adventures of Ducrot Pepys—full of high jinks superimposed by Tom's irrepressible good humor. One of his favorites was Tom standing atop his desk with a pillow stuffed in his [bath] robe, expounding on a variety of subjects a là "Senator Claghorn," the Al Capp character from the Li'l Abner comic strip. Tom demonstrated that he was a very smart guy as a cadet, but his love of life was too great to take himself or his intelligence too seriously.

Going into the Field Artillery, Tom served with the 7th Division Artillery in Japan following the basic course at Fort Sill, Oklahoma. He returned to Fort Sill for the advanced course and then served in the Korean War with the 58th Artillery Battalion of the 3rd Division. This was followed by assignments with the 11th Airborne Division at Fort Campbell, Kentucky, and the 8th Division in Germany. In this latter assignment, he was detailed as an advisor to the German Army and later served as a liaison officer to the British Army of the Rhine.

In 1961, Tom left active duty to try his hand at other things, but he stayed active in the Army Reserve. He later served several tours on active duty and graduated from C&GSC at Fort Leavenworth, Kansas, in 1964. He received the Legion of Merit for his work in the Reserves, particularly for his efforts with the Defense Civil Preparedness Agency.

Tom received a Master of Fine Arts from Catholic University in 1963, majoring in Drama and English Literature. This ... was a continuation of Tom's interests, as he had written a novel while on active duty. This book, entitled *King Julian*, had as its premise that George Washington had agreed to become America's king instead of president. He later wrote several plays, including musicals. One of his plays was produced in the Ford Theater in Washington.

In 1970, Tom took his first hot air balloon ride, an event that had far more significance than he could ever have believed at that time. One of Tom's sisters described him as enthusiastic, original, creative and imaginative. All of these descriptive terms came into play as Tom continued to delve into the realm of lighter-than-air flight. Ironically, Tom's father, as a young Naval officer, had been the chief investigating officer for the "Macon" dirigible disaster. Tom became a student and advocate of the use of the wind as a natural resource ... He had always been fascinated with the forces of nature and he began to contemplate the feasibility of pollution-free transportation ... He believed that man had to free himself from dependence on fossil fuels which were ruining the planet. To him, the harnessing of the energies of nature [would be] the salvation of the Earth ...

Tom's attempt to be the first person to cross the Atlantic by balloon was different from any previous approach. Vincent Lally, manager of the Global Atmosphere Measurements Program for the National Center for Atmospheric Research at Boulder, Colorado, said at the time: "All the others have been adventure flights. I feel this is the first attempt for an Atlantic crossing based on reasonable, technical grounds. Gatch is attempting to work with nature instead of working against it."

Unlike other [balloon] projects, Tom had no rich backers. For the attempt to cross the Atlantic he spent $60,000 of his own, plus two years of full-time work preparing his project, which he named *Light Heart*. He built the gondola at his home in Virginia. Six feet in diameter, extremely lightweight, it was insulated and also had the capability to "bounce off" radar if he was forced to ditch. The gondola was to be sealed and pressurized during its flight. Finally, at 1929 hours on

February 18, 1974, Tom Gatch stood in the hatch of the *Light Heart* and waved goodbye to his friends and family as they released the ropes that allowed the *Light Heart* to rise into the heavens. In the rigging of the gondola was a pennant from his father's battleship, the *South Dakota*.

That night and the next day, Tom floated on an easterly course. He consistently checked in with passing airliners at 35,000–36,000 feet. The final contact was with BOAC flight 583 at 1250 hours Tuesday, 19 February, 925 miles northeast of San Juan [Puerto Rico]. It was evident from the airliner's communication that the *Light Heart* was moving on a course far to the south of Tom's plots. Also, he was moving away from the most heavily traveled commercial air lanes. Through Tuesday night and Wednesday there were no reports from Tom nor any sightings. Tom's associates were not alarmed at this point, as they assumed that he was simply out of radio range. The Liberian freighter *Ore Meridian* spotted the *Light Heart* shortly after dawn on Tuesday, 1,000 miles west of the Canaries, even farther south than before. The *Meridian*'s report didn't reach his associates until Friday at noon. Now they were worried.

The *Meridian* reported an apparently lifeless balloon floating far off course at an unaccountably low altitude. Except for unproven balloon or life raft reports in scattered areas, no further information about Tom has been received since the *Meridian*'s sighting on February 21, 1974.

We will never know for sure what happened to our friend, classmate and brother. We do know that the world lost a remarkable man. His niece, Jocklyn Armstrong, wrote an article about Tom's flight ... She wrote: "Tom did more than think and dream; he used his own logic, and in areas where he did not have expertise, he consulted those [who] did. He listened and he dared. Tom's lifestyle rejected apathy and inertia. His drive had to do with freedom and going beyond himself. February 19, 1974, Tom Gatch lifted off in a small white sphere suspended under ten white balloons. He has disappeared. His determination and imagination have not."

One of Tom's roommates said, "Tom was a wonderful person and I am certain that he 'shed this mortal coil' in the fashion which matched his temperament—with a flair." Tom's family endowed a scholarship for an acolyte in the National Cathedral Choir in Tom's memory. This was done because Tom had a beautiful boy soprano voice and had spent two years as a choir member at St. Albans. At the memorial service, the Dean of the National Cathedral read from a credo that Tom carried in his wallet. It said, in part: "You are as young as your faith, as old as your debts. Live every day of your life as though you expect to live forever."

In reminiscing about Tom, one of his sisters said: "Little did I realize that someday I would enter the Smithsonian Air and Space Museum in Washington to see my young brother's balloon pictured on its beautiful take-off from Harrisburg, Pennsylvania, Airport. He was one of the balloon immortals."

Tom faced a different danger than we anticipated when we were cadets, but he faced it as we all knew he would. Tom Gatch has joined "The Long Grey Line." Those of us who remain behind can only say, "Well done, be thou at peace."

The only son in a family of three children, Tom Gatch set out to accomplish what others had then only dreamed of doing. What happened during his Atlantic crossing, as General McWhorter has pointed out, will never actually be known. However, there is a possibility that enclosed in his gondola he may have encountered a problem with his cabin pressurization system, resulting in a loss of oxygen and a subsequent loss of consciousness. This condition is called hypoxia.

I experienced hypoxia during a test in the Air Force. I was undergoing flight physiological training in a high altitude chamber. Part of the training was a simple coordination exercise—the moving of wooden pegs on a peg board. Six or eight of us were in the chamber, working in pairs. While we played with our peg boards, an attendant outside the chamber slowly lowered the oxygen pressure inside. At the first sign of difficulty in moving the pegs, we were told by the attendant to grab an oxygen mask and strap it on. I didn't properly heed the attendant, and found myself on the floor of the chamber, regaining consciousness with a mask shoved against my face. It all happened quickly—the only warning was a loss of clearheadedness and motor coordination just before blackout. Had others not been present to apply the oxygen mask, I never would have regained consciousness.

Tom Gatch reported early in his voyage that the portholes of the gondola were iced over, and the inside temperature was about forty degrees Fahrenheit. It is possible that as the voyage progressed ice formed in his cabin pressure regulator—the unit that supplies oxygen under pressure in a sealed environment. The ice might have blocked the system and cut off his supply. This could have occurred while Tom was asleep, in which case he would have had no indication at all of anything wrong. Alone in the gondola, Tom would have fallen unconscious and suffocated. The *Light Heart* would have drifted without a pilot, slowly losing altitude.

Whatever his fate, Tom Gatch did inspire others. His flight was followed by a series of attempts leading—four years later—to the first successful balloon crossing of the North Atlantic. The voyage of the *Light Heart* was thus not made in vain.

In July 1978, the hot-air balloon *Zanussi*, crewed by Donald Allan Cameron and Major Christopher Dafey, both of Great Britain, crossed the Atlantic from St. John's, Newfoundland, Canada, to the Bay of Biscay. The aeronauts only just failed to be the first to complete a crossing of the North Atlantic in a balloon (they were off by 103 miles). However, they set an endurance and distance record for a hot-air balloon that still stands—traveling 2,074.817 miles in ninety-six hours and twenty-four minutes.

A month later, aeronauts Ben Abruzzo and Maxie L. Anderson completed the first fully success-ful North Atlantic crossing. They lifted in the *Double Eagle II* from Presque Isle, Maine, on August 12, 1978, and set down in Miserey, France five days later, on August 17. The flight set a duration record of 137 hours, five minutes.

Ten years after Tom Gatch's attempt in the *Light Heart*, an Air Force colonel and expert skydiver made the first successful solo North Atlantic crossing. Joe Kittinger, who in 1960 completed the longest delayed parachute drop (16.04 miles from a balloon at 102,800 feet), lifted from Caribou, Maine on September 14, 1984, and four days later, on September 18, landed near Savona, Italy—completing a distance of 3,543 miles.

NOTES
94. Adi-Kent Thomas Jeffrey, *The Bermuda Triangle* (Pennsylvania: New Hope Publishing Company, 1973), p. 9.

95. Vincent H. Gaddis came up with the name "Bermuda Triangle" for the title of an article, "The Deadly Bermuda Triangle," published in the magazine *Argosy*, February 1964.

96. Ivan T. Sanderson, *Invisible Residents* (New York and Cleveland: World Publishing Company, 1970), pp. 166–168.

97. Robert J. Durant, "Vile Vortices, or a Disquisition on Certain Madness Maritime," *Pursuit*, July 1975, pp. 76–77.

98. Larry Kusche, *The Bermuda Triangle Mystery—Solved* (New York: Warner Books, 1975) pp. 107–129.

99. In a follow-up book published in 1980 by Harper & Row (*Vanished*, later renamed *The Disappearance of Flight 19*), Kusche—who is an instrument flight instructor—suggests that Taylor's navigational compasses may not have failed—that Taylor himself may have been at fault. He says (p. 161): "… a pilot's usual first reaction when he gets lost is to doubt his compass. It is tempting to have more confidence in terrain that looks familiar than in a compass that disagrees with the comforting landmarks."
   Taylor's radio transmissions left no doubt that he believed he was over the Florida Keys. However, direction finders eventually calculated the flight's position as north of the Bahamas and east of New Smyrna, Florida.

100. Author identified as 'X,' "Navy To Investigate Sunken Aircraft," *Pursuit*, Summer 1977, pp. 70–71.

101. Major Gen. John C. McWhorter, Jr., *A Chronicle of Duty, Honor, Country* (1993: self-published, P.O. Box 984, Kerrville, Texas 78029).

Afterword

On a cold, damp night in June 1977, I stood alongside a stretch of abandoned railroad tracks and stared at a motorized trolley loaded with electronic hardware. The location was an out-of-service Conrail track in northwestern New Jersey, where a group of researchers and engineers—members of an organization called Vestigia—were attempting to detect, photograph, and electronically measure a ghost. I had been invited to witness the experiment by my friend Raymond (see Foreword), who at the time was working closely with the group.

The ghost, in this case, was a recurrent phenomenon known as a "spooklight." There are more than fifty similar cases at known locations throughout the United States. Most are found along lonely rural lanes or near abandoned railroad tracks, though others are found in pasturelands or even near mountain tops. Usually there is a local legend that says the light was some unfortunate soul—carrying a lamp or a lantern—killed at that location.

At any rate, I found myself leaning against the trunk of a gnarled oak during the early morning of June 12, 1977. Over my jeans and heavy shirt I wore an old Army blanket, poncho style. A man named Joe was leaning against the opposite side of the tree, and we were both staring, with very tired eyes, at the rail trolley parked some fifteen feet away.

The trolley, constructed especially for the project, was equipped with infrared and ultraviolet detectors, motion picture and still cameras, and various other devices and instruments for measuring and recording light and energy. Beyond the trolley, on the far side of the tracks, was a truck trailer also laden with electronic gear. Several researchers crowded inside the trailer, monitoring gauges and instruments. Up and down the mile of abandoned track—three hundred yards in one direction, one thousand yards in the other—were more individuals standing watch. We had all been in place for hours and the frustration was mounting. There had been no spooklight, and no peep from any of the instruments.

What made the situation doubly frustrating was that on a previous occasion (November 20, 1976, at 10:21 P.M.) the team had not only encountered the light, but managed to photograph it with 35-mm infrared film. Frame by frame, the developed film revealed the light as a series of images, each different in size, intensity, and density as it coalesced and tightened in form while following a path just over the tracks. Of nearly equal interest, however, was the fact that the photos were taken by a man who could not even see the light!

The spooklight had appeared over the tracks in plain sight of one group of watchers, and should have been visible to another group which included the photographer, but for the second group, the light was simply not there! So the photographer aimed his camera and snapped pictures of apparent darkness, hoping something would show on the infrared film. Meanwhile, high radiation was registering on a Geiger counter. And an oscilloscope, wired directly to the tracks, displayed an electrical frequency in the range of forty thousand hertz.

That had been six months earlier. So far on this night we had netted only weariness and frustration. Then, around 1:30 A.M., something happened.

A small instrument on the trolley began to spark with a bluish light, not unlike a short-circuit. I pointed this out to Joe, who was nearly comatose at his side of the oak. Aroused and alarmed, he used a hand-held radio to contact one of the men inside the trailer, Bill Wagner, the designer of the trolley. Simultaneously, a man down the track monitoring a Geiger counter began shouting that he was getting high readings—nothing dangerous but unusual nonetheless. The readings, I later learned, had gone from a normal background of twenty to thirty counts per minute to sixty-five or seventy counts per minute.

Within the moment, the Vestigia crew had cranked up a motion picture camera on the trolley and engaged the trolley motor. Over Joe's radio I heard Bill Wagner explain that the ultraviolet sensor (the sparking instrument) was registering something invisible to the human eye. The trolley began moving, rolling down the track in the direction of the man with the Geiger counter.

Then, as abruptly as it had begun, it was over: the phenomenon was gone. The radiation readings fell to normal and the ultraviolet sensor stopped registering. The trolley was recalled and the camera reset. Once again, all was silent.

Throughout the remainder of the night the Geiger counter showed occasional high readings, but none approaching the earlier reading of sixty-five to seventy counts per minute. Just before dawn we began clearing the area, gathering up gear and supplies. Men staggered in from the various posts, their enthusiasm spent. Another night had passed in pursuit of the unknown.

The spooklight phenomenon, like UFOs, like skyquakes, or even like some of the accounts of strange creatures in the preceding chapters, is a puzzle without a real solution. We make guesses, of course. Over the years all sorts of pretenders to knowledge have offered some "certain" explanation or other for any, or all, of these phenomena.

UFOs, for example: the prevailing opinion is that unidentified flying objects are alien spacecraft manned by god-like, benevolent overseers who regard us in the same sense that we regard our pets—or gray-skinned, insect-eyed devils who abduct members of our species to hybridize with their own. There never has been conclusive proof of any of this. True, there are eyewitness accounts of "aliens" and "spacecraft," and the stories are often from credible people who are both frightened and awed by their experience. There are reports of "landed" craft and occupants who have spoken freely with witnesses; and there are reports (endless reports) of victims who have been medically probed and experimented upon by alien abductors. The reports are so numerous, in fact, that our Earth would seem to be swimming in aliens.

In some cases, the witness is physically marked or burned during the encounter. In other cases, traces of radiation or visible soil impressions remain at the site of the encounter. In still other cases, radar images and photographs help substantiate a UFO sighting. But are we really faced with something extraterrestrial? Or are we dealing with something else entirely?

The tales of classical mythology—Greek, Roman, and Norse —tell us that gods once strode the earth. Great in size and equally great in power, the divinities held sway over mankind, often acting cruelly or contemptuously in their dealings with mortal beings. At the same time, they occasionally demonstrated affection and even love for chosen individuals (such as Zeus's love for Callisto, or Apollo's love for Cassandra). With the coming of Christianity the classical gods were ultimately cast aside. Not so with another type of entity, always in the background, yet ever present: the diminutive people—the elves, fairies, and leprechauns of legend.

Tales of wee folk, while generally considered to be of Celtic origin, are actually global in scope. Strikingly similar stories have been passed down by Africans and Native Americans, Chinese and Australians, and by islanders in Hawaii, to name a few. Today, many individuals from many cultures still believe in the wee people (though any discussion of this is made with great care). The wee folk seem somehow bound to us and we to them. Like the old gods, the folklore about them suggests a disdain for men demonstrated in acts of mischief, balanced by occasional acts of love or amorous affection.

Perhaps the most heinous crime the wee people were said to commit was to spirit away the young and unwary to secret places in the forest or mountains. Sometimes the abductee experienced a loss of time. Minutes or hours might seem to pass in the fairy realm, but for friends and family of the missing person, elapsed time was actually measured in days or even weeks. Sometimes a member of the fairy folk developed a sexual or emotional attachment to a particular human, and procreation would occur (not all fairies or elves are said to be truly tiny in stature). The result was a "changeling" child. The computer scientist and astrophysicist, Dr. Jacques Vallee, writing in *Dimensions*,[102] offers a long documented history of sexual liaison between members of human and non-human races.

While stories of wee folk abducting, or procreating with, humans can easily be accepted within a framework of early folklore, they are less than acceptable amid the trappings of a technological society. Nevertheless, contemporary reports are common enough. They have been recounted in books such as Whitley Strieber's *Communion*. They have also been reported on network television, including a surprisingly objective April 1994 installment of the CBS News magazine "48 Hours." The difference between these and earlier accounts is that the contemporary abductions are not perceived in a classical sense. Rather, they are reported as a frightening encounter aboard a spaceship with small, grey-skinned aliens. It is the experience of *faerie* all over again; only the cultural frame of reference is different.

The belief that at least some aspects of the UFO phenomenon are a replay of classic fairy lore has been hotly debated in the UFO community. European researchers and many in the former Soviet Union openly support the theory, or at least remain open-minded. With few exceptions (among them the afore-mentioned Dr. Vallee), researchers in the United States tend to ignore or discount the idea entirely. They cite a lack of empirical, or observational, data in support of this and all occult views, while another position—known as the "psycho-social" theory—fares little better. And yet, with nothing more than empirical data to back their own beliefs (observation must be supported by some means of test, after all), United States researchers have promoted the ET explanation as the only plausible answer to the UFO mystery. This is wrong, as more than one solution may surely apply.

Possibly the UFO phenomenon, or some part of it, is a form of manifested consciousness—an intelligence apart from human mind and thought that has co-existed with us through the ages and communicates in mythic form ... showing up as gods, fairies, or space aliens. This view was strongly endorsed by John Keel in his landmark volume, *Operation Trojan Horse*.[103] Similar views have been pursued by Dr. Vallee in numerous books, and by the author Brad Steiger in volumes such as *Revelation—The Divine Fire* and *Gods of Aquarius*.

Or perhaps UFOs are a kind of visionary experience, more akin to dream than reality, though real enough to the perceivers. In theory, such phenomena are shaped by the psychological and social environment of the visionary—hence the "psycho-social" hypothesis.

Some UFOs (as well as the spooklight phenomenon) may be a form of visible energy—a purely natural occurrence that intrudes into our realm from some neighboring reality or continuum. This speculation is similar to that offered by Dr. David Rind (see Chapter Fourteen) as an explanation for the phenomenon of mystery booms and skyquakes. Furthermore, none of these possibilities does anything to preclude the extraterrestrial hypothesis—the idea that still other UFOs may in fact be alien spacecraft.

A variety of explanations must also be considered in order to attempt to account for the many mystery creatures described in preceding chapters. A few, the winged entities and man-beasts of Chapter Ten, seem to be drawn directly from someone's nightmare—a kind of psychic hologram but with mass and substance, similar to the "creature from the id" popularized in the 1956 film "Forbidden Planet."[104] Others—the phantom panthers of Chapter Seven—appear real enough. They leave tracks and scat and display evident behavioral traits, though these traits are often characterized by abnormal violence and butchery along with a marked intelligence. They behave, in fact, as though they don't belong here, as though they had just stepped in from somewhere else and are keenly aware they may maim or kill with impunity. Still others—the sasquatches, the black pumas, even the unidentified lake monsters—give strong indication of being indigenous to this world, though elusive and uncaught.

James Moseley once observed that UFOs and other Fortean phenomena are mysteries that most likely will never be solved because they are somehow "interrelated with the fundamental mysteries of human life: Where do we come from? Why are we here? Where, if anywhere, do we go next?"[105]

Allen Greenfield put it somewhat differently: "The greatest mistake ufologists and skeptics have made [in their search for answers] is that tendency, noted long ago by the immortal Charles Fort, to isolate any one thing from any other thing. The UFO mystery, seen in a vacuum, will always remain an unsolved enigma. But as the Rosicrucians tell us in their mysteries, *Nequaquam vacuum* ('a vacuum exists nowhere')."[106]

In the end, all views, all solutions must be considered, otherwise we emulate the dog chasing its tail: moving in pointless circles, in pursuit of mysteries beyond our ken.

NOTES

102. Jacques Vallee, *Dimensions* (New York: Ballantine Books, 1989), pp. 101–132.

103. John A. Keel, *UFOs: Operation Trojan Horse* (New York: G.P. Putnam's Sons, 1970). Keel and Vallee (the latter writing in *Passport To Magonia*, Chicago: Henry Regnery and Company, 1969) were perhaps the first to seriously explore the mythological, occult, and psychological content of the UFO phenomenon.

104. "Forbidden Planet", released in 1956 by MGM Studios, starred Walter Pidgeon, Anne Francis, and Leslie Nielsen. The film boasted story and special effects that still rate highly today (Walt Disney Studios reportedly created the animated "creature" sequences used throughout). The core of the film's story is the discovery of an alien technology that permits a man's most

primitive fears and desires to take form in reality—the "creature from the *id*," the *id* being the part of the psyche associated with primitive needs and bestial desires.

105. James W. Moseley, "Forty Years In Ufoology: Moseley Becomes A Self-Appointed Elder Statesman," *Saucer Smear*, January 10, 1993), pp. 1–3.

106. Allen H. Greenfield, in a letter to *Saucer Smear*, Vol. 40, No. 9, p. 6. Greenfield is the author of *Secret Cipher Of The UFOnauts* (Lilburn, Georgia: IllumiNet Press, 1994), a concise book linking the UFO phenomenon to occultism. Greenfield discusses many of the early players in both ufology and the occult, examines the related history, and concludes that a cipher exists enabling occultists to decode the antics of the UFO entities. What's more, he explains the cipher, laying it all out for the reader.

Glossary

Changeling: Webster's defines a changeling as a child secretly exchanged for another in infancy. In folk lore, a changeling is a human child abducted and raised among elves or fairies. A broader folk definition has it that changelings are the progeny of a union between humans and non-humans (such as elves, or more recently, aliens), with the children themselves being nearly human in appearance and able to move freely in the mortal world.

Cryptozoology: As defined by the Belgian zoologist Bernard Heuvelmans, cryptozoology is "... the scientific study of hidden animals, *i.e.*, of still unknown animal forms about which only testimonial and circumstantial evidence is available, or material evidence is considered insufficient by some." Additionally, cryptozoology encompasses a study of animals which are reported or found out of their normal habitat or territory, or of animals presumably extinct but which continue to be reported nonetheless.

Felid: Cat (from the family name, *felidae*).

Fishery: A body of water, or a portion of such, where fish or sea life are routinely caught.

Flap: An Air Force expression for any condition, situation, or state-of-being characterized by an advanced degree of confusion, but just short of actual panic. It also refers to a tremendous increase in activity (such as UFO or "strange creature" activity), occurring simultaneously in many different locations. A flap can last several days or several weeks.

Hybridize: The act of creating progeny from two different life forms, either through direct mating of genetically compatible species, or through artificial means. Some UFO researchers believe a hybrid alien-human species is being created by extraterrestrials who are abducting humans for that very purpose. Hybrid animal species are commonplace on Earth (an example being the mule, the offspring of a mare and a male donkey), though such progeny are themselves usually sterile and unable to reproduce.

Hominid: Bipedal primate (from the family name *hominidae*).

Id: One of three theoretical divisions of the unconscious human psyche (the other two being the ego and superego). Modern psychology has it that the id represents instinctual bestial desires.

Manimal: Reference to large hairy bipeds of an unknown origin or species, generally said to have glowing red eyes and a strong, disagreeable smell. Tracks found in areas where manimals occur are very large and three-toed.

Melanism (melanistic): Increased amount of black pigmentation, such as in animal hair or fur.

Metaphysical: Generally refers to the more abstruse philosophical sciences, but as used herein is a synonym for the word supernatural.

Newspaper Morgue: Collection of old newspaper records, retained on microfilm or in paper form, in a newspaper office or newsroom.

Paddlefish: A scaleless freshwater fish (*Polyodon spathula*) with a large paddle-shaped snout. Also known in some parts of the United States as the "spoonbill" or "spoonbill cat." The paddlefish is native to some of the Great Lakes and the Mississippi River system, and can grow to lengths of five and six feet and weigh up to 180 pounds. A relative of the American species is found in the large rivers of China.

Phantom Panther: Descriptive term for large anomalous cats that appear, wreak havoc, and disappear. Phantom panther reports are often accompanied by the discovery of tracks that are cat-like except for apparent claw-marks.

Synchronicity: The occurrence of distinctly separate events within a narrow period of time which, on the surface, appear coincidental but which nonetheless seem to have some unexplained connection or association. An example of this could be that you are reading a book and take note of an uncommon phrase or expression, only to hear that same phrase or expression uttered moments later by someone passing by.

The psychologist C. G. Jung believed that synchronicity was the manifestation of some undefined linking process, separate from causality (the relationship between cause and effect) and yet complementary to it.

UFO Community: Refers to the researchers, scientists, writers, and field investigators who are actively involved in a study of the UFO phenomenon.

Index

Index

Psychic Pets & Spirit Animals
True Stories from the Files of FATE Magazine
FATE Magazine
Editorial Staff

In spite of all our scientific knowledge about animals, important questions remain about the nature of animal intelligence. Now, a large body of personal testimony compels us to raise still deeper questions. Are some animals, like some people, psychic? If human beings survive death, do animals? Do bonds exist between people and animals that are beyond our ability to comprehend?

Psychic Pets & Spirit Animals is a varied collection from the past fifty years of the real-life experiences of ordinary people with creatures great and small. You will encounter psychic pets, ghost animals, animal omens, extraordinary human-animal bonds, pet survival after death, phantom protectors and the weird creatures of cryptozoology. Dogs, cats, birds, horses, wolves, grizzly bears—even insects—are the heroes of shockingly true reports that illustrate just how little we know about the animals we think we know best.

The true stories in *Psychic Pets & Spirit Animals* suggest that animals are, in many ways, more like us than we think—and that they, too, can step into the strange and unknowable realm of the paranormal, where all things are possible.

1-56718-299-2, 272 pp., mass market, softcover
$4.99

Extra-Terrestrials Among Us
George C. Andrews

According to a law already on the books, which may be activated whenever the government wishes to enforce it, anyone found guilty of E.T. contact is to be quarantined indefinitely under armed guard. Does that sound like the government doesn't take Extra-Terrestrials seriously? This book blows the lid off the government's cover-up about UFOs and their occupants, setting the stage for a "Cosmic Watergate."

Author George Andrews researched the evidence concerning E.T. intervention in human affairs for more than a decade before presenting his startling conclusions. *Extra-Terrestrials Among Us* is an exciting challenge to "orthodox" thinking and will certainly broaden your perception of the world we live in.

This well-written book presents fascinating and documented case histories of cattle mutilations, lights in the sky, circular flying machines, strange disappearances, objects falling from the sky and spontaneous combustion. You are given direct information as to why E.T.s are here, case history descriptions of the varying appearances, and what they are trying to accomplish. You will also learn how to determine whether an alien contact is beneficial or harmful.

Here also is the story of CIA involvement, Nazi contacts, Martian landings, and much more. If you believe in E.T.s, or if you're not really sure, *Extra-Terrestrials Among Us* will open you eyes to new worlds—some existing right here on earth!

0-87542-001-X, 304 pp., mass market, photos, illustrations
$4.95

Ghosts, Hauntings & Possessions
The Best of Hans Holzer, Book I
Edited by
Raymond Buckland

Now, a collection of the best stories from best-selling author and psychic investigator Hans Holzer—in mass market format! Accounts in *Ghosts, Hauntings & Possessions* include:

- A 37-year-old housewife from Nebraska was tormented by a ghost that drove phantom cars and grabbed her foot while she lay in bed at night. Even after moving to a different state, she could still hear heavy breathing.

- A psychic visited with the spirit of Thomas Jefferson at Monticello. What scandals surrounded his life that the history books don't tell us?

- Here is the exact transcript of what transpired in a seance confrontation with Elvis Presley—almost a year after his death!

- Ordinary people from all over the country had premonitions about the murders of John and Robert Kennedy. Here are their stories.

- What happened to the middle-aged woman who played with the Ouija board and ended up tormented and possessed by the spirit of a former boyfriend?

- Here is the report of Abraham Lincoln's prophetic dream of his own funeral. Does his ghost still roam the White House because of unfinished business?

These stories and many more will intrigue, spook and entertain readers of all ages.

0-87542-367-1, 288 pp., mass market

$5.99

ESP, Witches & UFOs:
The Best of Hans Holzer, Book II
Edited by
Raymond Buckland

In this exciting anthology, best-selling author and psychic investigator Hans Holzer explores true accounts of the strange and unknown: telepathy, psychic and reincarnation dreams, survival after death, psycho-ecstasy, unorthodox healings, Pagans and Witches, and Ufonauts. Reports included in this volume:

- Mrs. F. dreamed of a group of killers and was particularly frightened by the eyes of their leader. Ten days later, the Sharon Tate murders broke into the headlines. When Mrs. F. saw the photo of Charles Manson, she immediately recognized him as the man from her dream

- How you can use four simple "wish-fulfillment" steps to achieve psycho-ecstasy—turning a negative situation into something positive

- Several true accounts of miraculous healings achieved by unorthodox medical practitioners

- How the author, when late to meet with a friend and unable to find a telephone nearby, sent a telepathic message to his friend via his friend's answering service

- The reasons why more and more people are turning to Witchcraft and Paganism as a way of life

- When UFOs land: physical evidence vs. cultists

These reports and many more will entertain and enlighten all readers intrigued by the mysteries of life ... and beyond!

0-87542-368-X, 304 pp., mass market

$4.95